Book Title: Building an Information Technology Security Awareness and Training Program

Book Author: Mark Wilson; Joan Hash

Book Abstract: NIST Special Publication 800-50, Building An Information Technology Security Awareness and Training Program, provides guidance for building an effective information technology (IT) security program and supports requirements specified in the Federal Information Security Management Act (FISMA) of 2002 and the Office of Management and Budget (OMB) Circular A-130, Appendix III.The document identifies the four critical steps in the life cycle of an IT security awareness and training program: 1) awareness and training program design (Section 3); 2) awareness and training material development (Section 4); 3) program implementation (Section 5); and 4) post-implementation (Section 6).The document is a companion publication to NIST Special Publication 800-16, Information Technology Security Training Requirements: A Role- and Performance-Based Model. The two publications are complementary - SP 800-50 works at a higher strategic level, discussing how to build an IT security awareness and training program, while SP 800-16 is at a lower tactical level, describing an approach to role-based IT security training.

Citation: NIST SP - 800-50

Keyword: awareness; certification; design; develop; education; implement; maintain; metrics; training

NIST Special Publication 800-50

**National Institute of
Standards and Technology**
Technology Administration
U.S. Department of Commerce

Building an Information
Technology Security Awareness
and Training Program

Mark Wilson and Joan Hash

COMPUTER SECURITY

Computer Security Division
Information Technology Laboratory
National Institute of Standards and Technology
Gaithersburg, MD 20899-8933

October 2003

U.S. Department of Commerce

Donald L. Evans, Secretary

Technology Administration

Phillip J. Bond, Under Secretary for Technology

National Institute of Standards and Technology

Arden L. Bement, Jr., Director

Reports on Computer Systems Technology

The Information Technology Laboratory (ITL) at the National Institute of Standards and Technology (NIST) promotes the U.S. economy and public welfare by providing technical leadership for the Nation's measurement and standards infrastructure. ITL develops tests, test methods, reference data, proof of concept implementations, and technical analyses to advance the development and productive use of information technology. ITL's responsibilities include the development of technical, physical, administrative, and management standards and guidelines for the cost-effective security and privacy of sensitive unclassified information in Federal computer systems. This Special Publication 800-series reports on ITL's research, guidance, and outreach efforts in computer security, and its collaborative activities with industry, government, and academic organizations.

U.S. GOVERNMENT PRINTING OFFICE
WASHINGTON: 2003

For sale by the Superintendent of Documents, U.S. Government Printing Office
Internet: bookstore.gpo.gov — Phone: (202) 512-1800 — Fax: (202) 512-2250
Mail: Stop SSOP, Washington, DC 20402-0001

Authority

This document has been developed by the National Institute of Standards and Technology (NIST) in furtherance of its statutory responsibilities under the Federal Information Security Management Act (FISMA) of 2002, Public Law 107-347.

NIST is responsible for developing standards and guidelines, including minimum requirements, for providing adequate information security for all agency operations and assets, but such standards and guidelines shall not apply to national security systems. This guideline is consistent with the requirements of the Office of Management and Budget (OMB) Circular A-130, Section 8b(3), Securing Agency Information Systems, as analyzed in A-130, Appendix IV: Analysis of Key Sections. Supplemental information is provided A-130, Appendix III.

This guideline has been prepared for use by federal agencies. It may be used by nongovernmental organizations on a voluntary basis and is not subject to copyright. (Attribution would be appreciated by NIST.)

Nothing in this document should be taken to contradict standards and guidelines made mandatory and binding on federal agencies by the Secretary of Commerce under statutory authority. Nor should these guidelines be interpreted as altering or superseding the existing authorities of the Secretary of Commerce, Director of the OMB, or any other federal official.

> *Certain commercial entities, equipment, or materials may be identified in this document in order to describe an experimental procedure or concept adequately. Such identification is not intended to imply recommendation or endorsement by the National Institute of Standards and Technology, nor is it intended to imply that the entities, materials, or equipment are necessarily the best available for the purpose.*

TABLE OF CONTENTS

LIST OF FIGURES

Acknowledgements

We would like to express our thanks to George Bieber, Department of Defense; Carolyn Schmidt, NIST IT Security Office; Jaren Doherty, National Institutes of Health (NIH); Becky Vasvary, National Oceanographic and Atmospheric Administration (NOAA); Richard Stone, Internal Revenue Service (IRS); and Pauline Bowen, Richard Kissel, and Tanya Brewer-Joneas of NIST. We would also like to thank the NIST Technical Editor, Elizabeth Lennon, for editing this document.

Noteworthy contributions were also made by Ann L. Brown, Department of Health and Human Services (DHHS) Indian Health Service; Carolyn O'Connor, DHHS/Program Support Center (PSC); and Charles A. Filius, DHHS/PSC.

Finally, we wish to thank the members of the Executive Board of the Federal Information Systems Security Educators' Association (FISSEA) - Barbara Cuffie, Social Security Administration (SSA); Patricia Black, Treasury Department; and Dara Murray, DHHS/PSC.

Executive Summary

NIST Special Publication 800-50, *Building An Information Technology Security Awareness and Training Program,* provides guidance for building an effective information technology (IT) security program and supports requirements specified in the Federal Information Security Management Act (FISMA) of 2002 and the Office of Management and Budget (OMB) Circular A-130, Appendix III. A strong IT security program cannot be put in place without significant attention given to training agency IT users on security policy, procedures, and techniques, as well as the various management, operational, and technical controls necessary and available to secure IT resources. In addition, those in the agency who manage the IT infrastructure need to have the necessary skills to carry out their assigned duties effectively. Failure to give attention to the area of security training puts an enterprise at great risk because security of agency resources is as much a *human issue* as it is a technology issue.

Everyone has a role to play in the success of a security awareness and training program but agency heads, Chief Information Officers (CIOs), program officials, and IT security program managers have key responsibilities to ensure that an effective program is established agency wide. The scope and content of the program must be tied to existing security program directives and established agency security policy. Within agency IT security program policy, there must exist clear requirements for the awareness and training program.

The document identifies the four critical steps in the life cycle of an IT security awareness and training program:

Awareness and Training Program Design (Section 3): In this step, an agency wide needs assessment is conducted and a training strategy is developed and approved. This strategic planning document identifies implementation tasks to be performed in support of established agency security training goals.

Awareness and Training Material Development (Section 4): This step focuses on available training sources, scope, content, and development of training material, including solicitation of contractor assistance if needed.

Program Implementation (Section 5): This step addresses effective communication and roll out of the awareness and training program. It also addresses options for delivery of awareness and training material (web-based, distance learning, video, on-site, etc.).

Post-Implementation (Section 6): This step gives guidance on keeping the program current and monitoring its effectiveness. Effective feedback methods are described (surveys, focus groups, benchmarking, etc.).

The document also discusses three common models used in managing a security training function.

Centralized: All responsibility resides with a central authority (e.g., CIO and IT security program manager).

Partially Decentralized: Training policy and strategy lie with a central authority, but implementation responsibilities are distributed.

Fully Decentralized: Only policy development resides with a central authority, and all other responsibilities are delegated to individual agency components.

The type of model considered should be based on an understanding and assessment of budget and other resource allocation, organization size, consistency of mission, and geographic dispersion of the organization.

The document is a companion publication to NIST Special Publication 800-16, *Information Technology Security Training Requirements: A Role- and Performance-Based Model.* The two publications are complementary – SP 800-50 works at a higher strategic level, discussing how to build an IT security awareness and training program, while SP 800-16 is at a lower tactical level, describing an approach to role-based IT security training.

1. Introduction

Federal agencies and organizations cannot protect the confidentiality, integrity, and availability of information in today's highly networked systems environment without ensuring that all people involved in using and managing IT:

Understand their roles and responsibilities related to the organizational mission;

Understand the organization's IT security policy, procedures, and practices; and

Have at least adequate knowledge of the various management, operational, and technical controls required and available to protect the IT resources for which they are responsible.

As cited in audit reports, periodicals, and conference presentations, it is generally understood by the IT security professional community that people are one of the weakest links in attempts to secure systems and networks. The "people factor" - not technology - is key to providing an adequate and appropriate level of security. If people are the key, but are also a weak link, more and better attention must be paid to this "asset." A robust and enterprise wide awareness and training program is paramount to ensuring that people understand their IT security responsibilities, organizational policies, and how to properly use and protect the IT resources entrusted to them.

1.1 Purpose

This document provides guidelines for building and maintaining a comprehensive awareness and training program, as part of an organization's IT security program. The guidance is presented in a life-cycle approach, ranging from designing (Section 3), developing (Section 4), and implementing (Section 5) an awareness and training program, through post-implementation evaluation of the program (Section 6). The document includes guidance on how IT security professionals can identify awareness and training needs, develop a training plan, and get organizational buy-in for the funding of awareness and training program efforts. This document also describes how to:

Select awareness and training topics;

Find sources of awareness and training material;

Implement awareness and training material, using a variety of methods;

Evaluate the effectiveness of the program; and

Update and improve the focus as technology and organizational priorities change.

1.2 Audience

This guidance is intended to be useful to several key audiences in an organization, including, but not limited to: the CIO, the IT security program manager[1] and staff, managers (including system and application owners) and their contractors, and agency training coordinators. The success of an

---

[1] Under the Federal Information Security Management Act (FISMA) this position is titled Senior Agency Information Security Officer. While this guideline uses the term "IT security program manager," it is understood that organizations use a variety of terms to identify the person responsible for the department's or agency's IT security program. For example, some organizations use "information systems security manager," "information systems security officer," "automated data processing (ADP) security officer," "automated information systems (AIS) security officer," or "information assurance security officer." Regardless of the term used, the position (or role) being described is that of the person responsible for the organization's enterprisewide IT security program.

organization's awareness and training program, and that of the overall IT security program, depend on the ability of these people to work toward a common goal of protecting the organization's information and IT-related resources.

1.3 Scope

The scope of this guideline covers what an organization should do to design, develop, implement, and maintain an IT security awareness and training program, as a part of the IT security program. The scope includes awareness and training needs of all users of an organization's IT, from employees to supervisors and functional managers, to executive-level managers. The guideline also discusses professional development (i.e., professionalization) and certification issues – topics that continue to gain acceptance in organizations. While it mentions and defines IT security education, this document does not address the topic in-depth.

The document is a companion publication to NIST Special Publication 800-16, *Information Technology Security Training Requirements: A Role- and Performance-Based Model.* The two publications are complementary – SP 800-50 works at a higher strategic level, discussing how to build an IT security awareness and training program, while SP 800-16 is at a lower tactical level, describing an approach to role-based IT security training.

1.4 Policy

OMB Circular A-130, Appendix III, addresses training as an element of a system security plan for a general support system and as an element of an application security plan for a major application.[2] Regarding the training element of a system security plan, the Circular states, *"Ensure that all individuals are appropriately trained in how to fulfill their security responsibilities before allowing them access to the system. Such training shall ensure that employees are versed in the rules of the system . . . and apprise them about available technical assistance and technical security products and techniques. Behavior consistent with the rules of the system and periodic refresher training shall be required for continued access to the system."* The Circular states that as part of an application security plan, *"Before allowing individuals access to the application, ensure that all individuals receive specialized training focused on their responsibilities and the application rules. This may be in addition to the training required for access to a system. Such training may vary from a notification at the time of access (e.g., for members of the public using an information retrieval application) to formal training (e.g., for an employee that works with a high-risk application)."*

Additionally, the Federal Information Security Management Act (FISMA) of 2002 tasks the head of each agency with the responsibility to *"ensure that the agency has trained personnel sufficient to assist the agency in complying with (*these requirements*) and related policies, procedures, standards, and guidelines(.)"* FISMA also requires that the head of each agency *"delegate to the agency Chief Information Officer (CIO) (*or a comparable official*), the authority to ensure compliance with the requirements imposed on the agency, including . . . training and oversee personnel with significant responsibilities for information security . . . (.)"* FISMA also states that the required *"agency wide information security program"* shall include *"security awareness training to inform personnel, including contractors and other users of information systems that support the operations and assets of the agency, of:*

> *(i) information security risks associated with their activities; and*

---

[2] Knowing what security training is necessary for users, system/network administrators, and managers of a system or application will help the system or application owner/manager properly budget for those security-related needs.

(ii) their responsibilities in complying with agency policies and procedures designed to reduce these risks(.)"

Within the agency IT security program policy, there should be a clear and distinct section devoted to agency wide requirements for the awareness and training program. Topics documented within the awareness and training program policy should include roles and responsibilities, development of program strategy and a program plan, implementation of the program plan, and maintenance of the awareness and training program.

1.5   Roles and Responsibilities

While it is important to understand the policies that require agencies to develop and implement awareness and training, it is crucial that agencies understand who has responsibility for IT security awareness and training. This section identifies and describes those within an organization that have responsibility for IT security awareness and training.

Some organizations have a mature IT security program, while other organizations may be struggling to achieve basic staffing, funding, and support. The form that an awareness and training program takes can vary greatly from agency to agency. This is due, in part, to the maturity of that program.[3] One way to help ensure that a program matures is to develop and document IT security awareness and training responsibilities for those key positions upon which the success of the program depends.[4]

1.5.1 Agency   Head

Agency heads must ensure that high priority is given to effective security awareness and training for the workforce. This includes implementation of a viable IT security program with a strong awareness and training component. Agency heads should:

Designate a CIO;

Assign responsibility for IT security;

Ensure that an agency wide IT security program is implemented, is well-supported by resources and budget, and is effective; and

Ensure that the agency has enough sufficiently trained personnel to protect its IT resources.

1.5.2   Chief Information Officer

Chief Information Officers (CIOs) are tasked by the FISMA to administer training and oversee personnel with significant responsibilities for information security. CIOs should work with the agency IT security program manager to:

Establish overall strategy for the IT security awareness and training program;

Ensure that the agency head, senior managers, system and data owners, and others understand the concepts and strategy of the security awareness and training program, and are informed of the progress of the program's implementation;

---

[3] Differences in organizational culture are indicated by the placement of the IT security program, funding support, and access to and support by management. See Section 3.1 for examples of different awareness and training program models that can be implemented in an agency.

[4] IT security awareness and training responsibilities can be documented in agency policy, position descriptions, and where applicable, in performance or individual development plans.

Ensure that the agency's IT security awareness and training program is funded;

Ensure the training of agency personnel with significant security responsibilities;

Ensure that all users are sufficiently trained in their security responsibilities; and

Ensure that effective tracking and reporting mechanisms are in place.

1.5.3 Information Technology Security Program Manager

The IT security program manager has tactical-level responsibility for the awareness and training program. In this role, the program manager should:

Ensure that awareness and training material developed is appropriate and timely for the intended audiences;

Ensure that awareness and training material is effectively deployed to reach the intended audience;

Ensure that users and managers have an effective way to provide feedback on the awareness and training material and its presentation;

Ensure that awareness and training material is reviewed periodically and updated when necessary; and

Assist in establishing a tracking and reporting strategy.

1.5.4 Managers

Managers have responsibility for complying with IT security awareness and training requirements established for their users. Managers should:

Work with the CIO and IT security program manager to meet shared responsibilities;

Serve in the role of system owner and/or data owner, where applicable;[5]

Consider developing individual development plans (IDPs) for users in roles with significant security responsibilities;

Promote the professional development and certification of the IT security program staff, full-time or part-time security officers, and others with significant security responsibilities;

Ensure that all users (including contractors) of their systems (i.e., general support systems and major applications) are appropriately trained in how to fulfill their security responsibilities before allowing them access;

Ensure that users (including contractors) understand specific rules of each system and application they use; and

Work to reduce errors and omissions by users due to lack of awareness and/or training.

---

[5] Managers who serve as owners of general support systems and major applications have responsibility for the overall IT security of those systems and applications, including ensuring that all users are appropriately trained.

1.5.5 Users

Users are the largest audience in any organization and are the single most important group of people who can help to reduce unintentional errors and IT vulnerabilities. Users may include employees, contractors, foreign or domestic guest researchers, other agency personnel, visitors, guests, and other collaborators or associates requiring access. Users must:

Understand and comply with agency security policies and procedures;

Be appropriately trained in the rules of behavior for the systems and applications to which they have access;

Work with management to meet training needs;

Keep software/ applications updated with security patches; and

Be aware of actions they can take to better protect their agency's information. These actions include, but are not limited to: proper password usage, data backup, proper antivirus protection, reporting any suspected incidents or violations of security policy, and following rules established to avoid social engineering attacks and rules to deter the spread of spam or viruses and worms.

THIS PAGE INTENTIONALLY LEFT BLANK.

2. Components: Awareness, Training, Education

A successful IT security program consists of: 1) developing IT security policy that reflects business needs tempered by known risks; 2) informing users of their IT security responsibilities, as documented in agency security policy and procedures; and 3) establishing processes for monitoring and reviewing the program.[6]

Security awareness and training should be focused on the organization's entire user population. Management should set the example for proper IT security behavior within an organization. An awareness program should begin with an effort that can be deployed and implemented in various ways and is aimed at all levels of the organization including senior and executive managers. The effectiveness of this effort will usually determine the effectiveness of the awareness and training program. This is also true for a successful IT security program.

An awareness and training program is crucial in that it is *the* vehicle for disseminating information that users, including managers, need in order to do their jobs. In the case of an IT security program, it is *the* vehicle to be used to communicate security requirements across the enterprise.

An effective IT security awareness and training program explains proper rules of behavior for the use of agency IT systems and information. The program communicates IT security policies and procedures that need to be followed. This must precede and lay the basis for any sanctions imposed due to noncompliance. Users first should be informed of the expectations. Accountability must be derived from a fully informed, well-trained, and aware workforce.

This section describes the relationship between awareness, training, and education – the awareness-training-education continuum.

2.1 The   Continuum

Learning is a continuum; it starts with awareness, builds to training, and evolves into education. The continuum is illustrated in Figure 2-1. The continuum is further described in Chapter 2 of NIST Special Publication 800-16, *Information Technology Security Training Requirements: A Role- and Performance-Based Model*, available at http://csrc.nist.gov/publications/nistpubs/index.html.[7]

---

[6] An effective IT security awareness and training program can succeed only if the material used in the program is firmly based on agency IT security program policy and IT issue-specific policies. If policies are written clearly and concisely, then the awareness and training material – based on the policies – will be built on a firm foundation.

[7] The continuum is mentioned here and shown in Figure 2-1 to show the conceptual relationship between awareness, training, and education as described in NIST Special Publication 800-16. For the purposes of this guideline, clear boundaries are established between the three methods of learning.

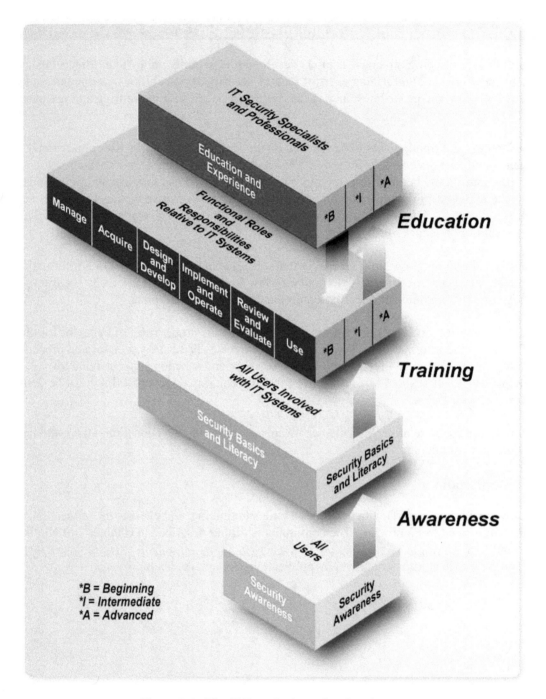

Figure 2-1: The IT Security Learning Continuum

2.2 Awareness

Security awareness efforts are designed to change behavior or reinforce good security practices. Awareness is defined in NIST Special Publication 800-16 as follows:

"Awareness is not training. The purpose of awareness presentations is simply to focus attention on security. Awareness presentations are intended to allow individuals to recognize IT security concerns and respond accordingly.

> Awareness is not training. The purpose of awareness presentations is simply to focus attention on security. Awareness presentations are intended to allow individuals to recognize IT security concerns and respond accordingly.

In awareness activities, the learner is the recipient of information, whereas the learner in a training environment has a more active role. Awareness relies on reaching broad audiences with attractive packaging techniques. Training is more formal, having a goal of building knowledge and skills to facilitate the job performance."

An example of a topic for an awareness session (or awareness material to be distributed) is virus protection. The subject can simply and briefly be addressed by describing what a virus is, what can happen if a virus infects a user's system, what the user should do to protect the system, and what the user should do if a virus is discovered. A list of possible awareness topics can be found in Section 4.1.1.

A bridge or transitional stage between awareness and training consists of what NIST Special Publication 800-16 calls *Security Basics and Literacy.* The basics and literacy material is a core set of terms, topics, and concepts. Once an organization has established a program that increases the general level of security awareness and vigilance, the basics and literacy material allow for the development or evolution of a more robust awareness program. It can also provide the foundation for the training program.

2.3 Training

Training is defined in NIST Special Publication 800-16 as follows: "The 'Training' level of the learning continuum strives to produce relevant and needed security skills and competencies by practitioners of functional specialties other than IT security (e.g., management, systems design and

> Training strives to produce relevant and needed security skills and competencies.

development, acquisition, auditing)." The most significant difference between training and awareness is that training seeks to teach skills, which allow a person to perform a specific function, while awareness seeks to focus an individual's attention on an issue or set of issues. The skills acquired during training are built upon the awareness foundation, in particular, upon the security basics and literacy material. A training curriculum must not necessarily lead to a formal degree from an institution of higher learning; however, a training course may contain much of the same material found in a course that a college or university includes in a certificate or degree program.

An example of training is an IT security course for system administrators, which should address in detail the management controls, operational controls, and technical controls that should be implemented. Management controls include policy, IT security program management, risk management, and life-cycle security. Operational controls include personnel and user issues, contingency planning, incident handling, awareness and training, computer support and operations, and physical and environmental security issues. Technical controls include identification and authentication, logical access controls, audit trails, and cryptography. (See NIST Special Publication 800-12, *An Introduction to Computer Security: The NIST Handbook,* for in-depth discussion of these controls (http://csrc.nist.gov/publications/nistpubs/index.html).)

2.4 Education

Education is defined in NIST Special Publication 800-16 as follows: *"The 'Education' level integrates all of the security skills and competencies of the various functional specialties into a common body of knowledge, adds a multidisciplinary study of concepts, issues, and principles (technological and social), and strives to produce IT security specialists and professionals capable of vision and pro-active response."*

> Education integrates all of the security skills and competencies of the various functional specialties into a common body of knowledge . . . and strives to produce IT security specialists and professionals capable of vision and pro-active response.

An example of education is a degree program at a college or university. Some people take a course or several courses to develop or enhance their skills in a particular discipline. This is training as opposed to education. Many colleges and universities offer certificate programs, wherein a student may take two, six, or eight classes, for example, in a related discipline, and is awarded a certificate upon completion. Often, these certificate programs are conducted as a joint effort between schools and software or hardware vendors. These programs are more characteristic of training than education. Those responsible for security training need to assess both types of programs and decide which one better addresses identified needs.

2.5 Professional   Development

Professional development is intended to ensure that users, from beginner to the career security professional, possess a required level of knowledge and competence necessary for their roles. Professional development validates skills through certification. Such development and successful certification can be termed "professionalization." The preparatory work to testing for such a certification normally includes study of a prescribed body of knowledge or technical curriculum, and may be supplemented by on-the-job experience.

The movement toward professionalization within the IT security field can be seen among IT security officers, IT security auditors, IT contractors, and system/network administrators, and is evolving. There are two types of certification: general and technical. The general certification focuses on establishing a foundation of knowledge on the many aspects of the IT security profession. The technical certification focuses primarily on the technical security issues related to specific platforms, operating systems, vendor products, etc.

Some agencies and organizations focus on IT security professionals with certifications as part of their recruitment efforts. Other organizations offer pay raises and bonuses to retain users with certifications and encourage others in the IT security field to seek certification.

3. Designing an Awareness and Training Program

There are three major steps in the development of an IT security awareness and training program – designing the program (including the development of the IT security awareness and training program plan), developing the awareness and training material, and implementing the program. Even a small amount of IT security awareness and training can go a long way toward improving the IT security posture of, and vigilance within, an organization. This section describes the first step in the development of an awareness and training program: designing the program.

Awareness and training programs must be designed with the organization mission in mind. It is important that the awareness and training program supports the business needs of the organization and be relevant to the organization's culture and IT architecture. The most successful programs are those that users feel are relevant to the subject matter and issues presented.

Designing an IT security awareness and training program answers the question "What is our plan for developing and implementing awareness and training opportunities that are compliant with existing directives?"[8] In the design step of the program, the agency's awareness and training needs are identified, an effective agency wide awareness and training plan is developed, organizational buy-in is sought and secured, and priorities[9] are established.

This section describes:

How to structure the awareness and training activity;

How to (and why) conduct a needs assessment;

How to develop an awareness and training plan;

How to establish priorities;

How to "set the bar" (i.e., the level of complexity of the subject matter) properly; and

How to fund the awareness and training program.

3.1 Structuring an Agency Awareness and Training Program

An awareness and training program may be designed, developed, and implemented in many different ways. Three common approaches or models are described below:

Model 1: Centralized policy, strategy, and implementation;

Model 2: Centralized policy and strategy, distributed implementation; and

Model 3: Centralized policy, distributed strategy and implementation.

The model that is embraced and established to oversee the awareness and training program activity depends on:

The size and geographic dispersion of the organization;

---

[8] The awareness and training plan should reflect the organization's strategy for meeting its awareness and training program responsibilities.

[9] Priorities include what awareness or training material will be developed first and who will be the first to receive the material.

11

Defined organizational roles and responsibilities; and

Budget allocations and authority.

Model 1: Centralized Program Management Model (Centralized Policy, Strategy, and Implementation)

In this model, responsibility and budget for the entire organization's IT security awareness and training program is given to a central authority. All directives, strategy development, planning, and scheduling is coordinated through this "security awareness and training" authority.

Figure 3-1: Model 1 – Centralized Program Management

Because the awareness and training strategy is developed at the central authority, the needs assessment – which helps determine the strategy – is also conducted by the central authority. The central authority also develops the training plan as well as the awareness and training material. The method(s) of implementing the material throughout the organization is determined and accomplished by the central authority. Typically, in such an organization, both the CIO and IT security program manager are organizationally located within this central authority.

Communication between the central authority and the organizational units travels in both directions. The central authority communicates the agency's policy directives regarding IT security awareness and training, the strategy for conducting the program, and the material and method(s) of implementation to the organizational units. The organizational units provide information requested by the central authority. For example, to meet its responsibilities, the central authority may collect data on the number of attendees at awareness sessions, the number of people trained on a particular topic, and the number of people yet to attend awareness and training sessions. The organizational unit can also provide feedback on the effectiveness of awareness and training material and on the appropriateness of the method(s) used to implement the material. This allows the central authority to fine-tune, add or delete material, or modify the implementation method(s).

This centralized program management model is often deployed by agencies that:

Are relatively small or have a high degree of structure and central management of most IT functions;

Have, at the headquarters level, the necessary resources, expertise, and knowledge of the mission(s) and operations at the unit level; or

Have a high degree of similarity in mission and operational objectives across all of its components.

Model 2: Partially Decentralized Program Management Model (Centralized Policy and Strategy; Distributed Implementation)

In this model, security awareness and training policy and strategy are defined by a central authority, but implementation is delegated to line management officials in the organization. Awareness and training budget allocation, material development, and scheduling are the responsibilities of these officials.

The needs assessment is conducted by the central authority, because they still determine the strategy for the awareness and training program. Policy, strategy, and budget are passed from the central authority to the organizational units. Based on the strategy, the organizational units develop their own training plans. The organizational units develop their awareness and training material, and determine the method(s) of deploying the material within their own units.

As was the case in the centralized program management model (Model 1), communication between the central authority and the organizational units travels in both directions in this model. The central authority communicates the agency's policy directives regarding IT security awareness and training, the strategy for conducting the program, and the budget for each organizational unit. The central authority may also advise the organizational units that they are responsible for developing training plans and for implementing the program, and may provide guidance or training to the organizational units so that they can carry out their responsibilities.

The central authority may require periodic input from each organizational unit, reporting the budget expenditures made, the status of unit training plans, and progress reports on the implementation of the awareness and training material. The central authority may also require the organizational units to report the number of attendees at awareness sessions, the number of people trained on a particular topic, and the number of people yet to attend awareness and training sessions. The organizational unit may be asked to describe lessons learned, so the central authority can provide effective guidance to other units.

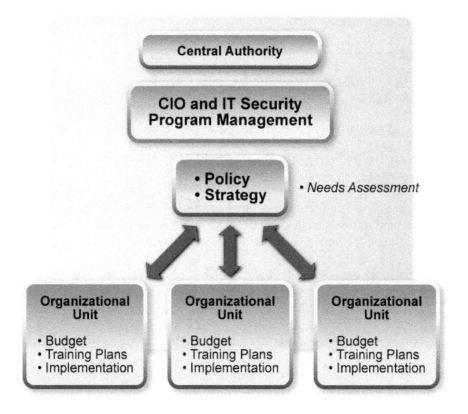

Figure 3-2: Model 2 - Partially Decentralized Program Management

This partially decentralized program management model is often deployed by agencies that:

Are relatively large or have a fairly decentralized structure with clear responsibilities assigned to both the headquarters (central) and unit levels;

Have functions that are spread over a wide geographical area; or

Have organizational units with diverse missions, so that awareness and training programs may differ significantly, based on unit-specific needs.

Model 3: Fully Decentralized Program Management Model (Centralized Policy; Distributed Strategy and Implementation)

In this model, the central security awareness and training authority (CIO/IT security program manager) disseminates broad policy and expectations regarding security awareness and training requirements, but gives responsibility for executing the entire program to other organizational units. This model normally uses a series of *distributed authority* directives, driven from the central authority. This normally means creation of a subsystem of CIOs and IT security program managers subordinate to the central CIO and IT security officer.

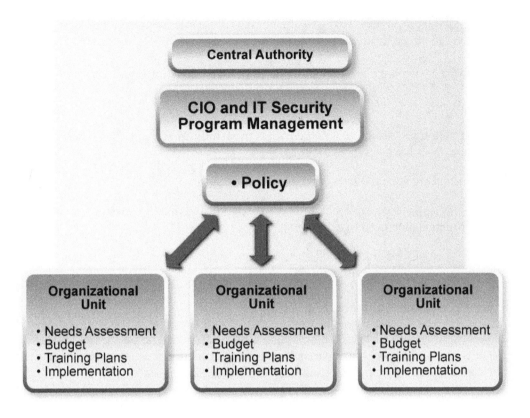

Figure 3-3: Model 3 – Fully Decentralized Program Management

The needs assessment is conducted by each organizational unit, because in this model, the units determine the strategy for the awareness and training program. Policy and budget are passed from the central authority to the organizational units. Based on the strategy, the organizational units develop their own training plans. The organizational units develop their awareness and training material, and determine the method(s) of deploying the material within their own units.

As was the case in the centralized program management model (Model 1) and the partially decentralized program management model (Model 2), communication between the central authority and the organizational units travels in both directions in this model. The central authority communicates the agency's policy directives regarding IT security awareness and training, and the budget for each organizational unit. The central authority may also advise the organizational units that they are responsible for conducting their own needs assessment, developing their strategy, developing training plans, and implementing the program. The central authority may provide guidance or training to the organizational units so that they can carry out their responsibilities.

> Unless the central authority has a very good strategy for policy and program requirement enforcement and can take into account performance and operational issues at the unit level, utilizing the fully decentralized program management model may be "throwing the IT security program over the wall" with little or no accountability.

The central authority may require periodic input from each organizational unit, reporting the budget expenditures made, the status and results of needs assessments, the strategy chosen by the organizational unit, the status of training plans, and progress reports on the implementation of the awareness and training material. The central authority may also require the organizational units to report the number of attendees at awareness sessions, the number of people trained on a particular topic, and the number of people yet to attend awareness and training sessions.

This fully decentralized program management model is often deployed by agencies that:

Are relatively large;

Have a very decentralized structure with general responsibilities assigned to the headquarters (central) and specific responsibilities assigned to unit levels;

Have functions that are spread over a wide geographical area; or

Have *quasi-autonomous* organizational units with separate and distinct missions, so that awareness and training programs may need to differ greatly.

Once the model to be employed is identified, the approach to conducting a needs assessment should be defined consistent with the organizational model selected.

3.2 Conducting a Needs Assessment

A needs assessment is a process that can be used to determine an organization's awareness and training needs. The results of a needs assessment can provide justification to convince management to allocate adequate resources to meet the identified awareness and training needs.

In conducting a needs assessment, it is important that key personnel be involved. As a minimum, the following roles should be addressed in terms of any special training needs:

Executive Management – Organizational leaders need to fully understand directives and laws that form the basis for the security program. They also need to comprehend their leadership roles in ensuring full compliance by users within their units.

Security Personnel (security program managers and security officers) – These individuals act as expert consultants for their organization and therefore must be well educated on security policy and accepted best practices.

System Owners – Owners must have a broad understanding of security policy and a high degree of understanding regarding security controls and requirements applicable to the systems they manage.

System Administrators and IT Support Personnel – Entrusted with a high degree of authority over support operations critical to a successful security program, these individuals need a higher degree of technical knowledge in effective security practices and implementation.

Operational Managers and System Users – These individuals need a high degree of security awareness and training on security controls and rules of behavior for systems they use to conduct business operations.

A variety of sources of information in an agency can be used to determine IT security awareness and training needs, and there are different ways to collect that information. Figure 3-4 suggests techniques for gathering information as part of a needs assessment.[10]

---

[10] The needs assessment process should only be as complex as is needed to identify an organization's awareness and training program needs. Similarly, the tools that are employed to identify those needs should be selected with an understanding of the organization's culture and conventions, as well as knowledge of the organization's size, workforce complexity, and

Interviews with all key groups and organizations identified

Organizational surveys

Review and assessment of available resource material, such as current awareness and training material, training schedules, and lists of attendees

Analysis of metrics related to awareness and training (e.g., percentage of users completing required awareness session or exposure, percentage of users with significant security responsibilities who have been trained in role-specific material)

Review of security plans for general support systems and major applications to identify system and application owners and appointed security representatives

Review of system inventory and application user ID databases to determine all who have access

Review of any findings and/or recommendations from oversight bodies (e.g., Congressional inquiry, inspector general, internal review/audit, and internal controls program) or program reviews regarding the IT security program

Conversations and interviews with management, owners of general support systems and major applications, and other organization staff whose business functions rely on IT

Analysis of events (such as denial of service attacks, website defacements, hijacking of systems used in subsequent attacks, successful virus attacks) might indicate the need for training (or additional training) of specific groups of people

Review when technical or infrastructure changes are made

The study of trends first identified in industry, academic, or government publications or by training/education organizations. The use of these "early warning systems" can provide insight into an issue within the organization that has yet to be seen as a problem.

Figure 3-4: Techniques for Gathering Information as Part of a Needs Assessment

Appendix A contains a sample needs assessment interview and questionnaire. (The sample provided contains some IT security-related questions as part of a general job-oriented questionnaire for system administrators. For situations in which the general job training requirements are known, the questionnaire can focus on the security awareness and training needs of the job.)

Metrics are an important and effective tool that can be used to help determine an agency's IT security awareness and training needs. Metrics monitor the accomplishment of the awareness and training program goals and objectives by quantifying the level of implementation of awareness and training and the effectiveness and efficiency of the awareness and training, analyzing the adequacy of awareness and training efforts, and identifying possible improvements. For a thorough discussion of metrics see NIST Special Publication 800-55, *Security Metrics Guide for Information Technology Systems.* A sample awareness and training metric is included in this document as Appendix B.

---

similarity or diversity of mission. For example, in a small agency with one mission or similar missions, the results of an IT security program review and/or an informal survey or questionnaire can usually be effective in identifying the awareness and training program needs. However, in a large agency with a diverse mix of users and missions, a more complex questionnaire may have to be developed to collect information that will be analyzed to identify program needs.

Figure 3-5 illustrates overarching agency-specific issues that must be understood at the start of the needs assessment. The techniques shown in Figure 3-4 should provide information that offers insight into, and understanding of, these issues. These issues should feed necessary information into the needs assessment process. Understanding them will help shape the strategy and design of the IT security awareness and training program.[11]

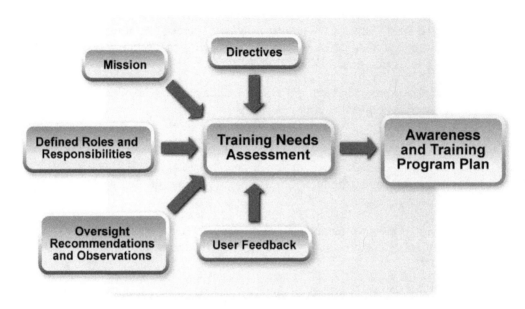

Figure 3-5: Understanding Overarching Agency-Specific Issues

Analysis of the information gathered should provide answers to key questions, shown in Figure 3-6.

What awareness, training, and/or education are needed (i.e., what is required)?

What is currently being done to meet these needs?

What is the current status regarding how these needs are being addressed (i.e., how well are current efforts working)?

Where are the gaps between the needs and what is being done (i.e., what more needs to be done)?

Which needs are most critical?

Figure 3-6: Key Questions to be Answered in Performing a Needs Assessment

Figure 3-7 shows the relationship between awareness and training requirements and an organization's current efforts. The shaded area represents the additional IT security awareness and/or training efforts

---

[11] Another issue that should be addressed during a needs assessment is the roles that have been identified as having significant security responsibilities. Existing roles that have been so identified should be reviewed to ensure that they still have significant security responsibilities. Other roles that previously have had little or no security responsibilities should also be reviewed. Organizational and technological changes in the organization may impact roles and the security responsibilities they carry.

that need to be made. The needs assessment can help identify these additional needs – the gap between what is currently being done and what is required.

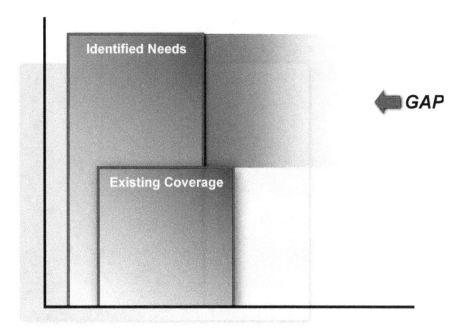

Figure 3-7: Required Awareness and Training Versus Current Effort

Another important aspect of a needs assessment is the related IT security awareness and training program requirements. For example, if awareness and training material will be presented utilizing computer-based training (CBT) technology, a technical assessment should be conducted on the organization's processing platform (e.g., local area network, workstations, video cards, speakers) to determine if the existing environment will support the new or expanded awareness and training program. Similarly, if the organization plans to provide classroom training, the needs assessment should identify if adequate space exists for an effective learning environment. There may also be Human Resources issues, including employees with disabilities and special needs. Labor union issues may also arise where they previously did not.

Once the needs assessment has been completed, information necessary to develop an awareness and training plan is available. The plan should cover the entire organization and incorporate priorities identified by the needs assessment.

3.3   Developing an Awareness and Training Strategy and Plan

Completion of the needs assessment allows an agency to develop a strategy for developing, implementing, and maintaining its IT security awareness and training program. The plan is the working document containing the elements that make up the strategy. The plan should discuss the following elements:

Existing national and local policy that requires the awareness and training to be accomplished;

Scope of the awareness and training program;

Roles and responsibilities of agency personnel who should design, develop, implement, and maintain the awareness and training material, and who should ensure that the appropriate users attend or view the applicable material;

Goals to be accomplished for each aspect of the program (e.g., awareness, training, education, professional development [certification]);

Target audiences for each aspect of the program;

Mandatory (and if applicable, optional) courses or material for each target audience;

Learning objectives for each aspect of the program;

Topics to be addressed in each session or course;

Deployment methods to be used for each aspect of the program;

Documentation, feedback, and evidence of learning for each aspect of the program;[12]

Evaluation and update of material for each aspect of the program; and

Frequency that each target audience should be exposed to material.[13]

Appendix C contains a sample awareness and training program plan template.

3.4 Establishing Priorities

Once the security awareness and training strategy and plan have been finalized, an implementation schedule must be established. If this needs to occur in phases (e.g., due to budget constraints and resource availability), it is important to decide the factors to be used in determining which initiative to schedule first and in what sequence. Key factors to consider are:

Availability of Material/Resources—If awareness and training material and necessary resources are readily available, key initiatives in the plan can be scheduled early. However, if course material must be developed and/or instructors must be identified and scheduled, these requirements should be considered in setting priorities.

Role and Organizational Impact—It is very common to address priority in terms of organizational role and risk. Broad-based awareness initiatives that address the enterprise wide mandate may receive high priority because the rules of good security practices can be delivered to the workforce quickly. Also, it is common to look at *high trust/high impact* positions (e.g., IT security program managers, security officers, system administrators, and security administrators whose positions in the organization have been determined to have a higher sensitivity) and ensure that they receive high priority in the rollout strategy. These types of positions are typically commensurate with the type of access (and to what system) these users possess.

State of Current Compliance – This involves looking at major gaps in the awareness and training program (e.g., gap analysis) and targeting deficient areas for early rollout.

Critical Project Dependencies – If there are projects dependent upon a segment of security training in order to prepare the necessary requirements for the system involved (e.g., new operating system,

---

[12] This element of the awareness and training plan should document how the organization will track who has been trained and who still requires training, how attendees can provide comments on the appropriateness of material, and how the agency will determine if the attendee benefits from exposure to the awareness or training material.

[13] At a minimum, the entire workforce should be exposed to awareness material annually. A continuous awareness program, using various methods of delivery throughout the year, can be very effective. Security training for groups of users with significant security responsibility (e.g., system and network administrators, managers, security officers) should be incorporated into ongoing functional training as needed.

firewalls, virtual private networks [VPNs]), the training schedule needs to ensure that the training occurs within the stipulated timeframe necessary to address these dependencies.

3.5 Setting the Bar

"Setting the bar" means that a decision must be made as to the complexity of the material that will be developed. The complexity must be commensurate with the role of the person who will undergo the learning effort. Material should be developed based on two important criteria: 1) the target attendee's position within the organization, and 2) knowledge of the security skills required for that position. The complexity of the material must be determined before development begins. Setting the bar applies to all three types of learning – awareness, training, and education.

When setting the bar for an awareness effort, the focus should be on the expected rules of behavior for using systems. These rules, which should come directly from agency policy, apply to everyone in the organization. As such, they should be explained clearly enough that there is no margin for confusion or misunderstanding. As an agency's awareness program matures, and most users have been exposed to the initial material, the bar can be raised. There are a number of ways to do this, including developing a basics and literacy course, following the guidance in Chapter 3 of NIST Special Publication 800-16. Raising the bar is discussed further in Section 6.

> Setting the bar means that a decision must be made as to the complexity of the material that will be developed; it applies to all three types of learning – awareness, training, and education.

Setting the bar correctly is even more critical when developing training material. Because *the goal of training is to produce relevant and needed skills and competencies* it is crucial that the needs assessment identify those individuals with significant IT security responsibilities, assess their functions, and identify their training needs. Training material should be developed that provides the skill set(s) necessary for attendees to accomplish the security responsibilities associated with their jobs. IT security training material can be developed at a beginning level for a person who is just learning a discipline (e.g., system administrator, web or e-mail server administrator, auditor). Material can be developed at an intermediate level for someone who has more experience, and therefore more responsibility, in a discipline. Advanced material can be developed for those "centers of excellence" or agency subject matter experts whose jobs incorporate the highest level of trust and an accompanying high level of IT security responsibility. Chapter 4 of NIST Special Publication 800-16 provides guidance on developing training material for these three levels of complexity, including learning objectives at each of the three levels to aid the training course developer[14].

Setting the bar for the education level of learning can be more difficult because curricula are developed by colleges and universities, and is impacted less in the short term by agency-specific needs. Once education needs have been identified within an organization, usually within the IT security office, a school that provides the needed learning can be found. An agency can "shop" for a local college or university whose certificate or degree program meets its needs or for a school that offers such a program through distance learning. As was the case with training material, a college or university should be selected because its curriculum meets the security needs of the agency personnel.

---

[14] Agencies may find commercial off-the-shelf (COTS) training material that can be used to meet the more advanced or complex training needs of their staff. Agencies will still have to define learning objectives for each role or group of people, and will have to do so for each level of complexity. The available COTS training can then be compared to what is required for each role to determine if the COTS training meets the agency's needs. The subject of vendor-provided training is further addressed in Section 4.

3.6 Funding the Security Awareness and Training Program

Once an awareness and training strategy has been agreed upon and priorities established, funding requirements must be added to the plan. A determination must be made regarding the extent of funding support to be allocated based on the implementation models discussed in Section 3.1. The agency CIO must send a clear message regarding expectations for compliance in this area. Approaches used to determine funding sources must be addressed by agencies based on existing or anticipated budget and other agency priorities. The security awareness and training plan must be viewed as a set of minimum requirements to be met, and those requirements must be supportable from a budget or contractual perspective. Contractual training requirements should be specified in binding documentation (e.g., memos of understanding (MOUs), contracts). Approaches used to express the funding requirement may include:

Percent of overall training budget;

Allocation per user by role (e.g., training for key security personnel and system administrators will be more costly than general security training for those in the organization not performing security-specific functions);

Percent of overall IT budget; or

Explicit dollar allocations by component based on overall implementation costs.

Problems in implementation of the security awareness and training plan may occur when security awareness and training initiatives are deemed to be lower in priority than other agency initiatives. It is the responsibility of the CIO to assess competing priorities and develop a strategy to address any shortfall in funding that may impact the agency's ability to comply with existing security training requirements. This may mean adjusting the awareness and training strategy to be more in line with available budget, lobbying for additional funding, or directing a reallocation of current resources. It may also mean that the implementation plan may be phased in over some predefined time period as funding becomes available.

4. Developing   Awareness and Training Material

Once the awareness and training program has been designed, supporting material can be developed. Material should be developed[15] with the following in mind:

"What behavior do we want to reinforce?" (awareness); and

"What skill or skills do we want the audience to learn and apply?" (training).

In both cases, the focus should be on specific material that the participants should integrate into their jobs. Attendees will pay attention and incorporate what they see or hear in a session if they feel that the material was developed specifically for them. Any presentation that "feels" canned – impersonal and so general as to apply to any audience – will be filed away as just another of the annual "we're here because we have to be here" sessions. An awareness and training program can be effective, however, if the material is interesting and current.[16]

At some point the question will be asked, "Am I developing awareness $_{or}$ training material?" Generally, since the goal of awareness material is simply to focus attention on good security practices, the message that the awareness effort sends should be short and simple. The message can address one topic, or it can address a number of topics about which the audience should be aware.

The awareness audience must include all users in an organization. The message to be spread through an awareness program, or campaign,[17] should make all individuals aware of their commonly shared IT security responsibilities. On the other hand, the message in a training class is directed at a specific audience. The message in training material should include everything related to security that attendees need to know in order to do their jobs. Training material is usually far more in-depth than material used in an awareness session or campaign.

4.1   Developing Awareness Material

The question to be answered when beginning to develop material for an organization wide awareness program or campaign is, "What do we want all agency personnel to be aware of regarding IT security?" The awareness and training plan should contain a list of topics. E-mail advisories, online IT security daily news websites, and periodicals are good sources of ideas and material. Agency policy, program reviews, internal audits, internal controls program reviews, self-assessments, and spot-checks can also identify additional topics to address.

---

[15]   Awareness and training material can be developed in-house, adapted from other agencies' or professional organizations' work, or purchased from a contractor/vendor. For information about contracting for services and products, see draft NIST Special Publication 800-35, *Guide to Information Technology Security Services* and draft NIST Special Publication 800-36, *Guide to Selecting Information Technology Security Products* For more extensive guidelines on contracting issues see draft NIST Special Publication 800-4A, *Security Considerations in Federal Information Technology Procurements – A Guide for Procurement Initiators, Contracting Officers, and IT Security Officials*

[16]   Changing peoples' attitudes and behavior in terms of IT security can be a challenging task. New security policies are often seen as conflicting with the way users have done their job for years. For example, departments and agencies that once operated with the full and open sharing of information are now being required to control access to, and dissemination of, that information. A technique that has been successfully used to acclimate users to these necessary changes is to begin an awareness module or session by discussing IT security issues in the context of personal life experiences (e.g., identify theft, inappropriate access to personal health or financial data, hacking incidents).

[17]   An organization may decide to mount a security awareness campaign to focus on a particular issue. For example, if users are becoming targets of social engineering attacks or a particular virus, an awareness campaign can be quickly implemented that uses various awareness techniques to "get the word out." Such a campaign differs from the normal implementation of an awareness program by the need for a timely dissemination of information on a particular topic or group of topics.

4.1.1 Selecting Awareness Topics

A significant number of topics can be mentioned and briefly discussed in any awareness session or campaign.[18] Topics may include:

Password usage and management – including creation, frequency of changes, and protection

Protection from viruses, worms, Trojan horses, and other malicious code – scanning, updating definitions

Policy – implications of noncompliance

Unknown e-mail/attachments

Web usage – allowed versus prohibited; monitoring of user activity

Spam

Data backup and storage – centralized or decentralized approach

Social engineering

Incident response – contact whom? "What do I do?"

Shoulder surfing

Changes in system environment – increases in risks to systems and data (e.g., water, fire, dust or dirt, physical access)

Inventory and property transfer – identify responsible organization and user responsibilities (e.g., media sanitization)

Personal use and gain issues – systems at work and home

Handheld device security issues – address both physical and wireless security issues

Use of encryption and the transmission of sensitive/confidential information over the Internet – address agency policy, procedures, and technical contact for assistance

Laptop security while on travel – address both physical and information security issues

Personally owned systems and software at work – state whether allowed or not (e.g., copyrights)

Timely application of system patches – part of configuration management

Software license restriction issues – address when copies are allowed and not allowed

Supported/allowed software on organization systems – part of configuration management

Access control issues – address least privilege and separation of duties

Individual accountability – explain what this means in the organization

Use of acknowledgement statements – passwords, access to systems and data, personal use and gain

---

[18] A thorough discussion of topics, organized as management, operational, and technical controls, can be found in NIST Special Publications 800-12, 800-18, and 800-26.

Visitor control and physical access to spaces – discuss applicable physical security policy and procedures, e.g., challenge strangers, report unusual activity

Desktop security – discuss use of screensavers, restricting visitors' view of information on screen (preventing/limiting "shoulder surfing"), battery backup devices, allowed access to systems

Protect information subject to confidentiality concerns – in systems, archived, on backup media, in hardcopy form, and until destroyed

E-mail list etiquette – attached files and other rules.

4.1.2 Sources of Awareness Material

There are a variety of sources of material on security awareness that can be incorporated into an awareness program. The material can address a specific issue, or in some cases, can describe how to begin to develop an entire awareness program, session, or campaign. Sources of timely material may include:

E-mail advisories issued by industry-hosted news groups, academic institutions, or the organization's IT security office;

Professional organizations and vendors;

Online IT security daily news websites;

Periodicals; and

Conferences, seminars, and courses.

Awareness material can be developed using one theme at a time or created by combining a number of themes or messages into a presentation. For example, a poster or a slogan on an awareness tool should contain one theme, while an instructor-led session or web-based presentation can contain numerous themes. (Dissemination techniques are covered in greater depth in Section 5.) Regardless of the approach taken, the amount of information should not overwhelm the audience. Brief mention of requirements (policies), the problems that the requirements were designed to remedy, and actions to take are the major topics to be covered in a typical awareness presentation.[19]

A more complex awareness presentation that incorporates basics and literacy material (see Chapter 3 of NIST Special Publication 800-16) should go into more depth on a particular subject. Because basics and literacy is the bridge between awareness and training, this additional level of detail and complexity is appropriate.

4.2 Developing Training Material

The question to be answered when beginning to develop material for a specific training course is, "What skill or skills do we want the audience to learn?" The awareness and training plan should identify an audience, or several audiences, that should receive training tailored to address their IT security responsibilities. NIST Special Publication 800-16, *Information Technology Security Training Requirements: A Role- and Performance-Based Model* (http://csrc.nist.gov/publications/nistpubs/index.html), contains a methodology for building training

---

[19] The NIST Computer Security Division website's awareness, training, education, and professional development pages http://csrc.nist.gov/ATE contain a number of links to government, industry, and academic sites that offer or sell both awareness and training material.

courses for a number of different audiences. The methodology in the NIST publication will be discussed in this section. Other sources of training courses and material will also be identified and discussed.

4.2.1   A Model for Building Training Courses: NIST Special Pub. 800-16

The methodology in NIST Special Publication 800-16 provides a useful tool with which to develop IT security training courses. This section provides background information on the purpose of the publication and describes how to use the methodology to develop training courses.

Purpose and Methodology: Special Publication 800-16 represents the IT security training needs in the current distributed computing environment, as opposed to the mainframe-oriented environment of the mid- to late-1980s. The document identifies 26 roles that have some degree of responsibility for IT security. Special Publication 800-16 provides flexibility in its methodology for extension of roles and other parameters to accommodate future technologies and organizational roles. The methodology also allows for training courses to be developed at the beginning, intermediate, and advanced levels of training. Sample learning objectives are provided for each level to guide the course developer. Agencies should consider using the publication to map needed training to new and existing roles that have significant IT security responsibilities.

Using the Special Publication to Develop a Training Course: NIST Special Publication 800-16 includes a number of resources that a course developer can use to build a training course. The resources are: the IT security learning continuum model, 26 roles and role-based matrices, 46 training matrix cells, 12 body of knowledge topics and concepts, 3 fundamental training content categories, and 6 functional specialties.

Once an audience has been identified as needing IT security training, Appendix E of the NIST Special Publication can be used to assist in course selection.[20] Agencies can tailor this approach based on specific positions used in their organizations. Appendix E contains 26 matrices, one for each of the 26 roles identified in the publication. Figure 4-1 provides a sample matrix for a course for system administrators.

---

[20]   Once training needs are identified, some agencies rely on curriculum builders – professional training development specialists – to develop the training material. Since training development specialists are usually not IT security professionals, the specialist will work closely with the IT security staff to ensure accuracy of the material as well as the proper level of complexity.

IT Security Training Matrix - *System Administrator*

Training Areas	Functional Specialities						
	A Manage	B Acquire	C Design and Develop	D Implement and Operate	E Review and Evaluate	F Use	G Other
1. Laws and Regulations				1D ✓			
2. Security Program							
2.1. Planning							
2.2. Management				2.2D ✓			
3. System Life Cycle Security							
3.1 Initiation				3.2D ✓			
3.2. Development				3.3D ✓			
3.3. Test and Evaluation				3.4D ✓			
3.4. Implementation			3.4C ✓	3.4D ✓			
3.5. Operations	3.5A ✓		3.5C ✓	3.5D ✓			
3.6. Termination				3.6D ✓			
4. Other							

Figure 4-1: Sample IT Security Training Matrix

Within each matrix, there are a number of cells that are used to build the course material. There are a total of 46 cells, but only specific cells are used for each course. Some course matrices have as few as 2 cells, and the course matrix for an IT security officer/manager uses all 46 cells. Most matrices use 7 to 10 cells.

The matrix is organized by six role categories – or functional specialties – relative to three fundamental training content categories – or training areas (i.e., laws and regulations, security program, and system life cycle security). The six role categories or functional specialties are:

Manage – This category is for individuals who manage IT-based functions in an organization.

Acquire – This category is for those individuals who are involved in the acquisition of IT products and/or services (e.g., serve on a source selection board to evaluate vendor proposals for IT systems). This is especially important for those who serve as a contracting officer's technical representative (COTR).

Design and Develop – This category is for those individuals who design and develop systems and applications.

Operate – This category is for those individuals who operate (administer) IT systems (e.g., web servers, e-mail servers, file servers, LANs, WANs, mainframes).

Review and Evaluate – This category is for individuals who review and evaluate (audit) IT functions as part of an organization's internal controls program, internal review, or an external audit program (e.g., inspector general).

Use – This category is for individuals who access IT resources and/or use IT to do their jobs.

Categories (or functional specialties) are arranged in each matrix along the top, from left to right. A placeholder exists in the seventh column, called "Other," designed to be used if an additional role category or functional specialty is developed. These six categories allow a training course to be tailor-fit to an audience and allow the course to address specific functions within a role. For example, a system administrator may manage the function or may administer (operate) a system or systems. Training course material should be organized by role – by an individual's job function – within the organization.

In Figure 4-1, the sample matrix for a system administrator course, ten cells will be developed into the course material. Each cell can be seen as a building block for the course material. In this example, most of the cells fall in the "Implement and Operate" specialty or column, because it is assumed that the system administrator will be running (operating) a system or systems. Because this course will address system management, design, and development, several of the ten cells are shown in those specialties or columns.

4.2.2   Sources of Training Courses and Material

The first step in determining sources of training material to build a course(s) is to decide if the material will be developed in-house or contracted out. If the agency has in-house expertise and can afford to allocate the necessary resources to develop training material and courses, NIST Special Publication 800-16 can be used.

Figure 4-2 contains some key issues to consider in making the decision to develop a course in-house or to outsource.

Do we have the in-house resources to do the job? This includes people with the right skills and enough people to do the work.

Is it more cost-effective to develop the material in-house versus outsourcing?

Is there a funding mechanism in place (budget)?

Do we have a person on staff that can serve as the contracting officer's technical representative (COTR) and effectively monitor contractor activity?

Does the agency have the necessary resources (e.g., funding and staff with necessary expertise) to maintain the material, if it is developed by a contractor?

Does the course content sensitivity preclude use of a contractor?

Does outsourcing allow for critical training delivery schedules to be met?

Figure 4-2: Key Questions – Develop Training Material In-house or Outsource?

If the agency decides to outsource its training course development, there are a number of vendors that offer "off-the-shelf" courses that are suitable for particular audiences or that can be developed for specific audiences. Prior to selecting a particular vendor, agencies should have a thorough understanding of their training needs and be able to determine if a prospective vendor's material meets their needs.

Maximizing Partnerships: Agencies have more options from which to choose than to simply decide if they will develop training course material with existing resources or outsource. Agencies can establish (or maximize existing) partnerships with other agencies to develop material or coordinate training events that meet their IT security training needs. For example, several agencies may combine resources and expertise and develop a training course for a particular audience. If agency-specific material is contained in, and limited to, a single module in the course, all involved agencies can use the majority of the material developed. Agencies would then have to modify or tailor-fit only the module that contains the agency-specific material.

Similarly, an agency might organize an IT security day or an annual or regional conference and announce that the events are open to other agencies' personnel. While the material presented might not match exactly what is needed by both agencies, it can be a fairly inexpensive way to meet some of a particular audience's training needs. If such an arrangement is made, a process must be established to allow each participating agency to track attendance, ensure applicability of the training material, determine accountability, and address other administrative and management issues.

Agencies can explore the use of training material that has been developed by other agencies and that can be edited inexpensively rather than developing a completely new course. Care should be taken that the available material is applicable to the intended audience, and that the material addresses what prospective attendees need to know to satisfy their IT security responsibilities.

Within an agency, IT security program managers can build new partnerships, or reinforce existing ones, with the organization's training function or with functional managers who coordinate or conduct their own training. Functional training developed in-house (e.g., financial applications, personnel management) often lacks adequate discussion of related IT security issues. Through a partnership, the IT security program manager can offer to review existing references to security in the training material, checking for completeness and accuracy. The IT security program manager can also assist the training or functional manager by developing a security module for that functional material that has no security component. The IT security program manager can also review contract specifications for functional training development to be outsourced, ensuring that the appropriate security issues are addressed in sufficient detail and complexity for the intended audience.

THIS PAGE INTENTIONALLY LEFT BLANK.

5. Implementing the Awareness and Training Program

An IT security awareness and training program should be implemented only after:

A needs assessment has been conducted;

A strategy has been developed;

An awareness and training program plan for implementing that strategy has been completed; and

Awareness and training material has been developed.

Figure 5-1 shows these key steps leading to the implementation of the awareness and training program.

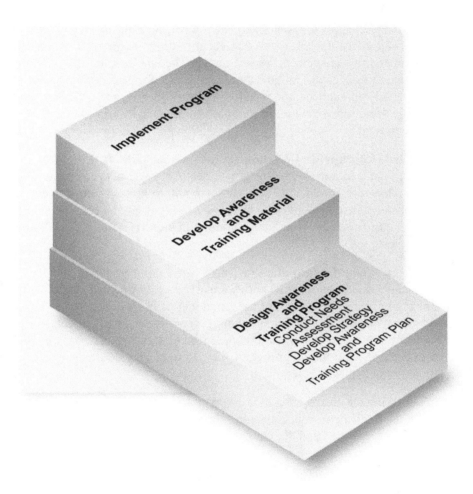

Figure 5-1: Key Steps Leading to Program Implementation

5.1 Communicating the Plan

The program's implementation must be fully explained to the organization to achieve support for its implementation and commitment of necessary resources. This explanation includes expectations of agency management and staff support, as well as expected results of the program and benefits to the organization. Funding issues must also be addressed. For example, agency managers must know if the cost to implement the awareness and training program will be totally funded by the CIO or IT security program budget, or if their budgets will be impacted to cover their share of the expense of implementing the program. It is essential that everyone involved in the implementation of the program understand their roles and responsibilities. In addition, schedules and completion requirements must be communicated.

Communication of the plan can be mapped to the three implementation models discussed in Section 3. Typical scenarios follow.

Centralized Program Model Communication Scenario: In this model, the CIO and/or IT security program manager develop all agency IT security awareness and training policy, develop the strategy and program plan, and implement the program. Therefore, all necessary funding for material development and implementation is controlled and provided by the CIO and IT security program manager. By the time the program is to be implemented, they have conducted the needs assessment, developed the training plan, and developed the awareness and training material. The CIO and/or IT security program manager should brief the agency head and senior management on the implementation plan and get approval to communicate it throughout the agency. Once the implementation plan is approved, the CIO and/or IT security program manager should communicate the plan to organizational unit management, providing the schedule for awareness and training offerings, and allocating slots in each session, where applicable, for each unit. The organizational unit managers should then communicate the plan to their staff, identify the awareness and training required, schedule attendees, and submit their nominations for each offering to the CIO or IT security program manager as required.

Partially Decentralized Program Model Communication Scenario: In this model, the CIO and/or the IT security program manager develop all agency IT security awareness and training policy and develop the strategy. They also conduct the needs assessment, from which the strategy is derived. Organizational unit managers are then given an awareness and training budget, develop training plans for their own unit, and implement the program. They should provide status reports to the CIO and/or IT security program manager as required.

Decentralized Program Model Communication Scenario: In this model, the CIO and/or IT security program manager disseminate broad policy and expectations regarding the IT security awareness and training program. Execution of the remainder of the program is the responsibility of the organizational units. The organizational unit managers are expected to conduct a needs assessment, formulate a strategy, develop a training plan, develop awareness and training material, and implement the awareness and training program. They should provide status reports to the CIO and/or IT security program manager as required.

Once the plan for implementing the awareness and training program has been explained to (and accepted by) agency management, the implementation can begin. There are a number of ways that awareness material and messages can be presented and disseminated throughout an organization.

5.2 Techniques for Delivering Awareness Material

Many techniques exist to get an IT security awareness message, or a series of messages, disseminated throughout an agency. The technique(s) chosen depend upon resources and the complexity of the message(s).

Techniques an agency may consider include, but are not limited to:

Messages on awareness tools (e.g., pens, key fobs, post-it notes, notepads, first aid kits, clean-up kits, diskettes with a message, bookmarks, Frisbees, clocks, "gotcha" cards)

Posters, "do and don't lists," or checklists

Screensavers and warning banners/messages

Newsletters

Desk-to-desk alerts (e.g., a hardcopy, bright-colored, one-page bulletin – either one per desk or routed through an office – that is distributed through the organization's mail system)

Agency wide e-mail messages

Videotapes

Web-based sessions

Computer-based sessions

Teleconferencing sessions

In-person, instructor-led sessions

IT security days or similar events

"Brown bag" seminars

Pop-up calendar with security contact information, monthly security tips, etc.

Mascots

Crossword puzzles

Awards program (e.g., plaques, mugs, letters of appreciation)

Some techniques that lend themselves to dissemination of a single message are the use of awareness tools, posters, access lists, screensavers and warning banners, desk-to-desk alerts, agency wide e-mail messages, brown bag seminars, and awards programs.

Techniques that can more easily include a number of messages include "do and don't lists," newsletters, videotapes, web-based sessions, computer-based sessions, teleconferencing sessions, in-person instructor-led sessions, and brown bag seminars.

Techniques that can be fairly inexpensive to implement include messages on awareness tools, posters, access lists, "do and don't lists," checklists, screensavers and warning banners, desk-to-desk alerts, agency wide e-mail messages, in-person instructor-led sessions, brown bag seminars, and rewards programs. Appendix D contains sample awareness posters.

Techniques that can require more resources include newsletters, videotapes, web-based sessions, computer-based sessions, and teleconferencing sessions.

In addition to making awareness material interesting and current, repeating an awareness message and using a variety of ways of presenting that message can greatly increase users' retention of awareness lessons or issues. For example, discussion in an instructor-led session about avoiding being a victim of a social engineering attack can be reinforced with posters, periodic agency wide e-mail messages, and messages on awareness tools that are distributed to users.

5.3   Techniques for Delivering Training Material

Techniques for effectively delivering training material should take advantage of technology that supports the following features:

Ease of use (e.g., easy to access and easy to update/maintain);

Scalability (e.g., can be used for various audience sizes and in various locations);

Accountability (e.g., capture and use statistics on degree of completion); and

Broad base of industry support (e.g., adequate number of potential vendors, better chance of finding follow-on support).

Some of the more common techniques that agencies can employ include:

Interactive video training (IVT) – IVT is one of several distance-learning techniques available for delivering training material. This technology supports two-way interactive audio and video instruction. The interactive feature makes the technique more effective than non-interactive techniques, but it is more expensive.

Web-based training – This technique is currently the most popular for distributed environments. "Attendees" of a web-based session can study independently and learn at their own pace. Testing and accountability features can be built in to gauge performance. Training models incorporating this technique are beginning to provide the additional benefit of interaction between instructor and student or among students.

Non-web, computer-based training – This technique continues to be popular even with web availability. It can still be an effective method for distribution of training material, especially if access to web-based material is not feasible. Like web-based training, this technique does not allow for interaction between the instructor and students or among students.

Onsite, instructor-led training (including peer presentations and mentoring) – This is one of the oldest, but one of the most popular techniques for delivering training material to an audience. The biggest advantage of the technique is the interactive nature of the instruction. This technique, however, has several potential disadvantages. In a large organization, there may be difficulty in scheduling sufficient classes so that all of the target audience can attend. In an organization that has a widely distributed workforce, there may be significant travel costs for instructors and students. Although there are challenges for distributed environments, some learners prefer this traditional method over other methods.

Blending various training delivery techniques in one session can be an effective way to present material and hold an audience's attention. For example, showing videos during an instructor-led session allows the audience to focus on a different source of information. The video can also reinforce what the instructor has been presenting. IVT, web-based training, and non-web, computer-based training can also be used as part of an instructor-led training session.

6. Post-Implementation

An organization's IT security awareness and training program can quickly become obsolete if sufficient attention is not paid to technology advancements, IT infrastructure and organizational changes, and shifts in organizational mission and priorities. CIOs and IT security program managers need to be cognizant of this potential problem and incorporate mechanisms into their strategy to ensure the program continues to be relevant and compliant with overall objectives.

Continuous improvement should always be the theme for security awareness and training initiatives, as this is one area where "*you can never do enough.*"

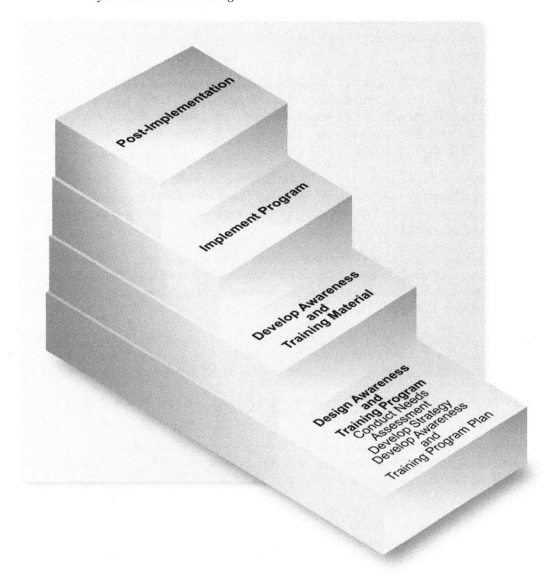

Figure 6-1: Key Steps Leading to Post-Implementation

6.1 Monitoring   Compliance

Once the program has been implemented, processes must be put in place to monitor compliance and effectiveness. An automated tracking system should be designed to capture key information regarding program activity (e.g., courses, dates, audience, costs, sources). The tracking system should capture this data at an agency level, so that it can be used to provide enterprise wide analysis and reporting regarding awareness, training, and education initiatives. Requirements for the database should incorporate the needs of all intended users. Typical users of such a database would include:

CIOs – Can use the database to support strategic planning, inform the agency head and other senior management officials on the health of the IT security awareness and training program, identify in-house capability and critical needs in security workforce, perform program analysis, identify activity enterprise wide, assist in security and IT budgeting, identify the need for program improvement, and assess compliance.

IT Security Program Managers – Can use the database to support security planning, provide status reports to the CIO and other management and security personnel, justify requests for funding, demonstrate compliance with agency-established goals and objectives, identify vendors and other training sources, respond to security-related inquiries, identify current coverage, and make adjustments for critical omissions.

Human Resource Departments – Can use the database to ensure that an effective mechanism exists for capturing all security-related training, identify IT security training related costs, assist in the establishment of position descriptions, support status reporting, respond to training inquiries, and aid in professional development.

Agency Training Departments – Can use the database to assist in developing overall agency training strategy, establish training database requirements tied to security directives, identify possible training sources, support training requests, identify course relevance and popularity, support budgeting activity, and respond to inquiries.

Functional Managers – Can use the database to monitor their user's training progress and adjust user training plans as needed, get status reports and respond to inquiries regarding security training in their components, and identify training sources and costs to assist with budget requests and proposals.

Auditors – Can use information from the database to monitor compliance with security directives and agency policy.

Chief Financial Officers (CFOs) – Can use information from the database to respond to budget inquiries, assist in financial planning, and provide reports to the agency head and senior managers regarding security training funding activities.

Tracking compliance involves assessing the status of the program as indicated by the database information and mapping it to standards established by the agency. Reports can be generated and used to identify gaps or problems. Corrective action and necessary follow-up can then be taken. This may take the form of formal reminders to management; additional awareness, training, or education offerings; and/or the establishment of a corrective plan with scheduled completion dates.

6.2   Evaluation and Feedback

Formal evaluation and feedback mechanisms are critical components of any security awareness, training, and education program. Continuous improvement cannot occur without a good sense of how the existing program is working. In addition, the feedback mechanism must be designed to address objectives initially established for the program. Once the baseline requirements have been solidified, a feedback strategy can be designed and implemented. Figure 6-2 shows various evaluation and feedback mechanisms that can be used to update the awareness and training program plan.[21]

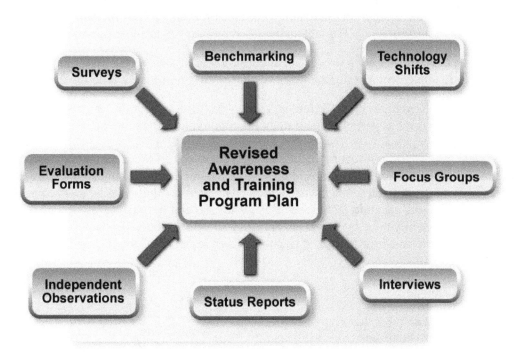

Figure 6-2: Evaluation and Feedback Techniques

A feedback strategy needs to incorporate elements that will address quality, scope, deployment method (e.g., web-based, onsite, offsite), level of difficulty, ease of use, duration of session, relevancy, currency, and suggestions for modification.

Many methods can be applied to solicit feedback. The most common include:

Evaluation Forms/Questionnaires – A variety of formats can be used. The best designs eliminate the need for a lot of writing on the part of the person completing them. The key is to design the forms to be as "user friendly" as possible. Work with the in-house experts who are familiar with the best techniques for designing these evaluation instruments or seek the assistance of outside experts.

Focus Groups – Bring subjects of the training together in open forums to discuss their perspectives on the IT security training program effectiveness and solicit their ideas for improvement.

Selective Interviews – This approach first identifies training target groups based on impact, priority, or other established criteria and identifies specific areas for feedback. Normally conducted using one-on-one interviews or in small homogeneous groupings (usually ten or less), this approach is more

---

[21] The awareness and training program plan represents the results of the design phase of the awareness and training program. The design phase is the first of the four major phases (i.e., design the program, develop material, implement the program, maintain the program) in the life cycle of an awareness and training program. Evaluation and feedback techniques can provide insights that should result in an update of the awareness and training program plan. As subsequent needs assessments are performed, it will be important to consider the insights gained from evaluation and feedback techniques, as a needs assessment helps an organization determine its awareness and training program plan.

personalized and private than the focus group approach and may encourage participants to be more forthcoming in their critique of the program.

Independent Observation/Analysis – Another approach for soliciting feedback is to incorporate a review of the IT security awareness and training program as a task to an outside contractor or other third party as part of an agency-initiated audit. The agency would do this in addition to the normal oversight activity (e.g., OIG, GAO) to get an unbiased opinion regarding program effectiveness.

Formal Status Reports – A good way to keep focus on security awareness and training requirements agency wide is to implement a requirement for regular status reporting by functional managers.

Security Program Benchmarking (External View) – Many organizations incorporate *"Security Program"* benchmarking as part of their strategy for continuous improvement and striving for excellence. *This type of benchmarking is focused on the question: How do I rate among my peers?* The *externally focused* form of security benchmarking compares an organization's performance against a number of other organizations and provides a report back to the agency on where they fall based on observed baselines across all organizations with data currently available. A component of this type of benchmarking should include security awareness and training. This type of benchmarking is normally done by experts in benchmarking techniques who have extensive information (data) across a broad range of organizations over a fairly long duration (five years or more).

6.3 Managing   Change

It will be necessary to ensure that the program, as structured, continues to be updated as new technology and associated security issues emerge. Training needs will shift as new skills and capabilities become necessary to respond to new architectural and technology changes. A change in the organizational mission and/or objectives can also influence ideas regarding how best to design training venues and content.

> Managing change is the component of the program designed to ensure that training/ awareness/education deployments do not become stagnant and therefore irrelevant to real emerging issues faced by the organization. It is also designed to address changes in security policy and procedures reflected in the culture of the agency.

Emerging issues, such as homeland defense, will also impact the nature and extent of security awareness activities necessary to keep users informed/educated about the latest exploits and countermeasures. New laws and court decisions may also impact agency policy that, in turn, may affect the development and/or implementation of awareness and training material. Finally, as security directives change or are updated, awareness and training material should reflect these changes.

6.4   Ongoing Improvement ("Raising the Bar")

This stage of the program is focused on creating a level of security awareness and excellence that achieves a pervasive security presence in the organization. The processes that deliver awareness, training, and education to the workforce should be totally integrated into the overall business strategy. A mature security awareness and training program defines a set of metrics for this area, and automated systems should be in place to support the capture of quantitative data and delivery of management information to accountable parties on a regular, predefined cycle.

Monitoring, follow-up, and corrective procedures are well defined and seamless. Finally, in this stage, agencies have incorporated into their awareness and training program formal mechanisms for ongoing research in areas of technology advancement, good practices, and benchmarking opportunities.

6.5 Program Success Indicators

CIOs, program officials, and IT security program managers should be primary advocates for continuous improvement and for supporting an agency's security awareness, training, and education program. It is critical that everyone be capable and willing to carry out their assigned security roles in the organization. In security, the phrase, "Only as strong as the weakest link," is true. Securing an organization's information and infrastructure is a $team$ effort. Listed below are some key indicators to gauge the support for, and acceptance of, the program.

Sufficient funding to implement the agreed-upon strategy.

Appropriate organizational placement to enable those with key responsibilities (CIO, program officials, and IT security program manager) to effectively implement the strategy.

Support for broad distribution (e.g., web, e-mail, TV) and posting of security awareness items.

Executive/senior level messages to staff regarding security (e.g., staff meetings, broadcasts to all users by agency head).

Use of metrics (e.g., to indicate a decline in security incidents or violations,[22] indicate that the gap between existing awareness and training coverage and identified needs is shrinking, the percentage of users being exposed to awareness material is increasing, the percentage of users with significant security responsibilities being appropriately trained is increasing).

Managers do not use their status in the organization to avoid security controls that are consistently adhered to by the rank and file.

Level of attendance at mandatory security forums/briefings.

Recognition of security contributions (e.g., awards, contests).

Motivation demonstrated by those playing key roles in managing/coordinating the security program.

---

[22] While improved security behavior can result in a decline in incidents or violations, reporting of potential incidents may increase because of enhanced vigilance among users.

APPENDIX A—SAMPLE NEEDS ASSESSMENT INTERVIEW AND QUESTIONNAIRE

Current Assignment (Agency/Office): _____

Parent Organization (Department/Agency): _____

Rank or Grade: _____ **Date of Current Assignment** (mm/yy): _____

JobTitle: _____

This questionnaire is designed to find out about the knowledge, skills, and experience you use to administer your organization's automated information systems and networks. It asks about functions you perform, how you learned to do them, and the kinds of training you think would be of greatest benefit to you on the job. The information you provide will be used to design security training to meet the needs of (agency name) system administrators. The questionnaire should take you approximately 30 minutes to complete.

Part 1. Background:

1. Do you currently perform duties as a system administrator?.............................**Yes No**
    1a. If yes, do you do the job on a full-time basis?..**Yes No**
    1b. If less than full time, what percent of time do you spend doing
        system administration duties? ...._____ **%**

2. How long have you worked as a system administrator?   _____ **Years   Months**

3. Do you have system administrators working for you?.......................................**Yes No**

4. Do you work for a system administrator?...**Yes No**

5. Did you have formal training in system administration?...................................**Yes No**
    (If Yes, please specify below)

(School or Vendor)	Course Title/Name	(Duration- Days) (Year)

(School or Vendor)	Course Title/Name	(Duration- Days) (Year)

6. Did you have formal training in system security? (If Yes, please specify below)...**Yes   No**

(School or Vendor)	Course Title/Name	(Duration- Days) (Year)

(School or Vendor)	Course Title/Name	(Duration- Days) (Year)

7. Please indicate the number of years of formal education you have completed.
    (e.g., HS =12 years, BA/BS= 16 years): _____

8. How many seminars or conferences relating to system administration or information
    systems security have you attended in the last year? _____

9. Do you regularly read computer/networking/software journals or magazines? (If yes,
    please specify below)..**Yes No**

Part 2. Task Performance and Training:

For each task in column A, circle the letter in column B that indicates how often you perform the task: O – *never* L – *less than once a month* M – *monthly* W – *weekly* D – *daily* **A B**		Put a check indicating the primary way you received your training to do this task. If "Other," please specify (e.g., workshops, trial and error, etc.).	For each task, indicate ( ) the level of training you feel you need Entry (E), Intermediate (I), Advanced (A)
Manage System Hardware:			
Plan hardware installation	O L M W D	__Class room ___ OJT (on the job) __ Self Study ___ Other _____	E ____ I____ A ____
Acquire hardware	O L M W D	__Class room ___ OJT __ Self Study ___ Other _____	E ____ I____ A ____
Coordinate network installation	O L M W D	__ Class room ___ OJT __ Self Study ___ Other	E ____ I____ A ____
Schedule preventive maintenance	O L M W D	__ Class room ___ OJT __ Self Study ___ Other	E ____ I____ A ____
Coordinate hardware repair	O L M W D	__Class room ___ OJT __ Self Study ___ Other _____	E ____ I____ A ____
Install hardware	O L M W D	__Class room ___ OJT __ Self Study ___ Other _____	E ____ I____ A ____
Boot system	O L M W D	__Class room ___ OJT __ Self Study ___ Other _____	E ____ I____ A ____
Maintain inventory of system hardware	O L M W D	__Class room ___ OJT __ Self Study ___ Other	E ____ I____ A ____
Order consumable supplies	O L M W D	__Class room ___ OJT __ Self Study ___ Other	E ____ I____ A ____
Run diagnostics	O L M W D	__Class room ___ OJT __ Self Study ___ Other _____	E ____ I____ A ____
Relocate hardware	O L M W D	__Class room ___ OJT __ Self Study ___ Other _____	E ____ I____ A ____
Manage System Software:			
Optimize operating system parameters	O L M W D	__Class room ___ OJT __ Self Study ___ Other _____	E ____ I____ A ____
Plan system changes	O L M W D	__Class room ___ OJT __ Self Study ___ Other _____	E ____ I____ A ____
Set system defaults	O L M W D	__Class room ___ OJT __ Self Study ___ Other _____	E ____ I____ A ____
Generate new operating system kernel	O L M W D	__Class room ___ OJT __ Self Study ___ Other	E ____ I____ A ____
Maintain system startup/shutdown procedures	O L M W D	__Class room ___ OJT __ Self Study ___ Other _____	E ____ I____ A ____
Maintain command files	O L M W D	__Class room ___ OJT __ Self Study ___ Other _____	E ____ I____ A ____
Test update validity	O L M W D	__Class room ___ OJT __ Self Study ___ Other _____	E ____ I____ A ____

For each task in column A, circle the letter in column B that indicates how often you perform the task: **O** – *never* **L** – *less than once a month* **M** – *monthly* **W** – *weekly* **D** – *daily*		Put a check indicating the primary way you received your training to do this task. If "Other," please specify (e.g., workshops, trial and error, etc.).	For each task, indicate ( ) the level of training you feel you need Entry (E), Intermediate (I), Advanced (A)
A B			
Install system software	O L M W D	__Class room ___ OJT Self Study Other	E ____ I____ A ____
Shut down system	O L M W D	__Class room ___ OJT Self Study Other	E ____ I____ A ____
Reboot system	O L M W D	__Class room ___ OJT Self Study Other	E ____ I____ A ____
Maintain software inventory	O L M W D	__Class room ___ OJT Self Study Other	E ____ I____ A ____
Install system changes	O L M W D	__Class room ___ OJT Self Study Other	E ____ I____ A ____
Install vendor-specific hardware	O L M W D	__Class room ___ OJT Self Study Other	E ____ I____ A ____
Install system updates or patches	O L M W D	__Class room ___ OJT Self Study Other	E ____ I____ A ____
Maintain documentation	O L M W D	__Class room ___ OJT Self Study Other	E ____ I____ A ____
Maintain Data Storage:			
Plan data storage layout	O L M W D	__Class room ___ OJT Self Study Other	E ____ I____ A ____
Plan backup procedures	O L M W D	__Class room ___ OJT Self Study Other	E ____ I____ A ____
Implement backup procedures	O L M W D	__Class room ___ OJT Self Study Other	E ____ I____ A ____
Monitor data storage use	O L M W D	__Class room ___ OJT Self Study Other	E ____ I____ A ____
Maintain file system integrity	O L M W D	__Class room ___ OJT Self Study Other	E ____ I____ A ____
Audit file system security	O L M W D	__Class room ___ OJT Self Study Other	E ____ I____ A ____
Delete unnecessary files	O L M W D	__Class room ___ OJT Self Study Other	E ____ I____ A ____
Manage log files	O L M W D	__Class room ___ OJT Self Study Other	E ____ I____ A ____
Maintain data storage layout	O L M W D	__Class room ___ OJT Self Study Other	E ____ I____ A ____
Format storage media	O L M W D	__Class room ___ OJT Self Study Other	E ____ I____ A ____
Partition disks	O L M W D	__Class room ___ OJT Self Study Other	E ____ I____ A ____
Create a file system	O L M W D	__Class room ___ OJT Self Study Other	E ____ I____ A ____
Load data	O L M W D	__Class room ___ OJT Self Study Other	E ____ I____ A ____
Restore data from a backup	O L M W D	__Class room ___ OJT Self Study Other	E ____ I____ A ____

For each task in column A, circle the letter in column B that indicates how often you perform the task: **O** – *never* **L** – *less than once a month* **M** – *monthly* **W** – *weekly* **D** – *daily* **A B**		Put a check indicating the primary way you received your training to do this task. If "Other," please specify (e.g., workshops, trial and error, etc.).	For each task, indicate ( ) the level of training you feel you need Entry (E), Intermediate (I), Advanced (A)
Manage Application Software:			
Evaluate effect of software packages	O L M W D	__Class room ___ OJT Self Study Other	E____ I____ A____
Optimize application parameters	O L M W D	__Class room ___ OJT Self Study Other	E____ I____ A____
Plan application changes	O L M W D	__Class room ___ OJT Self Study Other	E____ I____ A____
Ensure compatibility among applications	O L M W D	__Class room ___ OJT Self Study Other	E____ I____ A____
Allocate system resources to applications	O L M W D	__Class room ___ OJT Self Study Other	E____ I____ A____
Validate integrity of applications before installation	O L M W D	__Class room ___ OJT __ Self Study ___ Other _____	E____ I____ A____
Test validity of software installation	O L M W D	__Class room ___ OJT Self Study Other	E____ I____ A____
Install application software	O L M W D	__Class room ___ OJT Self Study Other	E____ I____ A____
Maintain inventory	O L M W D	__Class room ___ OJT Self Study Other	E____ I____ A____
Maintain application documentation	O L M W D	__Class room ___ OJT Self Study Other	E____ I____ A____
Install application updates	O L M W D	__Class room ___ OJT Self Study Other	E____ I____ A____
Plan network connectivity	O L M W D	__Class room ___ OJT Self Study Other	E____ I____ A____
Request interhost connectivity	O L M W D	__Class room ___ OJT Self Study Other	E____ I____ A____
Acquire Internet address	O L M W D	__Class room ___ OJT Self Study Other	E____ I____ A____
Build network cables	O L M W D	__Class room ___ OJT Self Study Other	E____ I____ A____
Configure TTY lines	O L M W D	__Class room ___ OJT Self Study Other	E____ I____ A____
Configure peripheral lines	O L M W D	__Class room ___ OJT Self Study Other	E____ I____ A____
Configure file servers and clients	O L M W D	__Class room ___ OJT Self Study Other	E____ I____ A____
Configure firewalls	O L M W D	__Class room ___ OJT Self Study Other	E____ I____ A____
Monitor network activity	O L M W D	__Class room ___ OJT Self Study Other	E____ I____ A____
Manage network services	O L M W D	__Class room ___ OJT Self Study Other	E____ I____ A____

For each task in column A, circle the letter in column B that indicates how often you perform the task: O – *never* L – *less than once a month* M – *monthly* W – *weekly* D – *daily*		Put a check indicating the primary way you received your training to do this task. If "Other," please specify (e.g., workshops, trial and error, etc.).	For each task, indicate ( ) the level of training you feel you need Entry (E), Intermediate (I), Advanced (A)
A B			
Manage network bridges and routers	O L M W D	__Class room ___ OJT Self Study Other	E ____ I ____ A ____
Manage print servers	O L M W D	__Class room ___ OJT Self Study Other	E ____ I ____ A ____
Manage terminal servers	O L M W D	__Class room ___ OJT Self Study Other	E ____ I ____ A ____
Manage network topology	O L M W D	__Class room ___ OJT Self Study Other	E ____ I ____ A ____
Assign addresses to nodes	O L M W D	__Class room ___ OJT Self Study Other	E ____ I ____ A ____
Install network software	O L M W D	__Class room ___ OJT Self Study Other	E ____ I ____ A ____
Set access permissions	O L M W D	__Class room ___ OJT Self Study Other	E ____ I ____ A ____
Start network software	O L M W D	__Class room ___ OJT Self Study Other	E ____ I ____ A ____
Test communication connectivity	O L M W D	__Class room ___ OJT Self Study Other	E ____ I ____ A ____
Stop network software	O L M W D	__Class room ___ OJT Self Study Other	E ____ I ____ A ____
Re-establish host connectivity	O L M W D	__Class room ___ OJT Self Study Other	E ____ I ____ A ____
Help establish audit guidelines	O L M W D	__Class room ___ OJT Self Study Other	E ____ I ____ A ____
Help establish user security guidelines	O L M W D	__Class room ___ OJT Self Study Other	E ____ I ____ A ____
Assist writing system security plans	O L M W D	__Class room ___ OJT Self Study Other	E ____ I ____ A ____
Assist in host network accreditation	O L M W D	__Class room ___ OJT Self Study Other	E ____ I ____ A ____
Ensure output labeling procedures	O L M W D	__Class room ___ OJT Self Study Other	E ____ I ____ A ____
Ensure data labeling procedures	O L M W D	__Class room ___ OJT Self Study Other	E ____ I ____ A ____
Assist testing security mechanisms	O L M W D	__Class room ___ OJT Self Study Other	E ____ I ____ A ____
Assist in analysis of audit trails	O L M W D	__Class room ___ OJT Self Study Other	E ____ I ____ A ____
Assist in incident handling	O L M W D	__Class room ___ OJT Self Study Other	E ____ I ____ A ____
Enforce security procedures	O L M W D	__Class room ___ OJT Self Study Other	E ____ I ____ A ____
Assist in maintaining physical security for the system	O L M W D	__Class room ___ OJT __ Self Study ___ Other _____	E ____ I ____ A ____

For each task in column A, circle the letter in column B that indicates how often you perform the task: **O** – *never* **L** – *less than once a month* **M** – *monthly* **W** – *weekly* **D** – *daily* **A B**		Put a check indicating the primary way you received your training to do this task. If "Other," please specify (**e.g.**, workshops, trial and error, etc.).	For each task, indicate ( ) the level of training you feel you need Entry (E), Intermediate (I), Advanced (A)
Assist in maintaining device access controls	O L M W D	__Class room ___ OJT __Self Study Other	E ____ I ____ A ____
Report security incidents	O L M W D	__Class room ___ OJT __Self Study Other	E ____ I ____ A ____
Manage Accounts:			
Plan account management strategy	O L M W D	__Class room ___ OJT __Self Study Other	E ____ I ____ A ____
Establish user login environments	O L M W D	__Class room ___ OJT __Self Study Other	E ____ I ____ A ____
Assist ISSO in managing mandatory access controls	O L M W D	__Class room ___ OJT __ Self Study ___ Other _____	E ____ I ____ A ____
Manage account privileges	O L M W D	__Class room ___ OJT __Self Study Other	E ____ I ____ A ____
Audit account activity	O L M W D	__Class room ___ OJT __Self Study Other	E ____ I ____ A ____
Manage resources used by account	O L M W D	__Class room ___ OJT __Self Study Other	E ____ I ____ A ____
Add new accounts	O L M W D	__Class room ___ OJT __Self Study Other	E ____ I ____ A ____
Assist in setting the account's access control list	O L M W D	__Class room ___ OJT __ Self Study ___ Other _____	E ____ I ____ A ____
Explain basic operating procedures	O L M W D	__Class room ___ OJT __Self Study Other	E ____ I ____ A ____
Assist in modifying passwords	O L M W D	__Class room ___ OJT __Self Study Other	E ____ I ____ A ____
Delete accounts	O L M W D	__Class room ___ OJT __Self Study Other	E ____ I ____ A ____
Troubleshoot Problems:			
Recreate problem scenarios	O L M W D	__Class room ___ OJT __Self Study Other	E ____ I ____ A ____
Interpret error messages	O L M W D	__Class room ___ OJT __Self Study Other	E ____ I ____ A ____
Test components	O L M W D	__Class room ___ OJT __Self Study Other	E ____ I ____ A ____
Isolate problems	O L M W D	__Class room ___ OJT __Self Study Other	E ____ I ____ A ____
Maintain log of problems and solutions	O L M W D	__Class room ___ OJT __Self Study Other	E ____ I ____ A ____
Recover from system crashes	O L M W D	__Class room ___ OJT __Self Study Other	E ____ I ____ A ____
Respond to user identified problems	O L M W D	__Class room ___ OJT __Self Study Other	E ____ I ____ A ____

For each task in column A, circle the letter in column B that indicates how often you perform the task: **O** – *never* **L** – *less than once a month* **M** – *monthly* **W** – *weekly* **D** – *daily* **A B**		Put a check indicating the primary way you received your training to do this task. If "Other," please specify (e.g., workshops, trial and error, etc.).	For each task, indicate ( ) the level of training you feel you need Entry (E), Intermediate (I), Advanced (A)
Gather troubleshooting information	O L M W D	__Class room ___ OJT Self Study Other	E ____ I____ A ____
Use diagnostic tools	O L M W D	__Class room ___ OJT Self Study Other	E ____ I____ A ____
Initiate corrective action	O L M W D	__Class room ___ OJT Self Study Other	E ____ I____ A ____

Part 2. Task Performance and Training (cont.):

Use the table below to indicate any other system administration functions you perform that are not covered above. For each, indicate how often you perform the task, the primary way you were trained to do the job, and whether you think more training would help you do the task.

For each task in column A, circle the letter in column B that indicates how often you perform the task: **O** – *never* **L** – *less than once a month* **M** – *monthly* **W** – *weekly* **D** – *daily* **A B**		Put a check indicating the primary way you received your training to do this task. If "Other," please specify (e.g., workshops, trial and error, etc.).	Indicate ( ) the level of training you feel you need Entry (E), Intermediate (I), Advanced (A)
	O L M W D	__ Class room ___ OJT __ Self Study ___ Other _____	E ____ I____ A ____
	O L M W D	__Class room ___ OJT __ Self Study ___ Other _____	E ____ I____ A ____
	O L M W D	__Class room ___ OJT __ Self Study ___ Other _____	E ____ I____ A ____
	O L M W D	__Class room ___ OJT Self Study Other	E ____ I____ A ____
	O L M W D	__Class room ___ OJT Self Study Other	E ____ I____ A ____
	O L M W D	__Class room ___ OJT __ Self Study ___ Other _____	E ____ I____ A ____
	O L M W D	__Class room ___ OJT __ Self Study ___ Other _____	E ____ I____ A ____
	O L M W D	__Class room ___ OJT __ Self Study ___ Other _____	E ____ I____ A ____

Part 3. Job Task Discussion:

1. Are you required to:
    ___Install firewalls?
    ___Operate firewalls?
    ___Maintain firewalls?

2. If you checked any responses in question 1, please specify:
    The number of firewalls _____,
    The type of hardware _____, and
    What software you work with_____

3. Are you required to install:
    ___Network cables
    ___PC's/Workstations
    ___Routers/Bridges
    ___Security-related hardware
    ___Security-related software
    ___Other software

4. Does your job require you to know how to program or write shell scripts? **Yes   No**
    In which language(s)?_____

5. What kinds of functions/programs have you written in the last year?
    ___ cron jobs
    ___ login functions
    ___ backups
    ___ restore
    ___ accounting functions
    ___ other (Please specify)_____

6. What kinds of scripts or programs do you maintain?
    ___ cron jobs
    ___ login functions
    ___ backups
    ___ restore
    ___ accounting functions
    ___ other (Please specify)_____

7. Do you share system duties with any of the following (Indicate the number of each)? ___Network Administrator(s)
    ___Database Administrator(s)
    ___Other SA(s)
    ___ISSO/ISSM(s)

8. Do you administer more than one network?......................................**Yes   No**

9. What operating systems and versions are used in your system? (e.g., Solaris 2.5.1)

    _____

10. Are you responsible for system security?.......................................**Yes** **No**
    If Yes, what instruction or policy defines that duty?_____
    _____

11. What specific programs do you use for each of the following (for each, please indicate if its use is optional (**O**) or required (**R**) by your command or organization):
    Network mapping_____
    Intrusion detection_____
    System logging_____
    Audit functions_____
    Password checking or enhancement_____

12. Are you a certified system administrator?.......................................**Yes** **No**
    If Yes, what specific training courses (classroom, CDs, CBTs, etc.) did you take to be certified?
    _____
    _____
    _____
    _____

13. What do you feel are your top five information system security training needs? (for each, indicate whether your need is for basic, intermediate or advanced training)
    A._____
    B._____
    C._____
    D._____
    E._____

    Additional comments:
    _____
    _____
    _____
    _____
    _____
    _____
    _____
    _____

    Thank you for participating in this survey.

THIS PAGE INTENTIONALLY LEFT BLANK.

APPENDIX B—SAMPLE AWARENESS AND TRAINING METRIC

Critical Element	13.1 Have employees received adequate training to fulfill their security responsibilities?
Subordinate Question	13.1.2 Are employee training and professional development documented and monitored?
Metric	The percentage of employees with significant security responsibilities who have received specialized training
Purpose	To gauge the level of expertise among designated security roles and security responsibilities for specific systems within the agency
Implementation Evidence	1. Are significant security responsibilities defined, with qualifications criteria, and documented? Yes ڤ No ڤ 2. Are records kept of which employees have specialized security responsibilities? Yes ڤ No ڤ 3. How many employees in your agency (or agency component, as applicable) have significant security responsibilities? _____ 4. Are training records maintained? (Training records indicate the training that specific employees have received.) Yes No 5. Do training plans state that specialized training is necessary? Yes ڤ No ڤ 6. How many of those with significant security responsibilities have received the required training stated in their training plan? _____ 7. If all personnel have not received training, state all reasons that apply: Insufficient funding Insufficient time ڤ Courses unavailable ڤ Employee has not registered ڤ _____ (Other (specify ڤ
Frequency	Annually, at a minimum
Formula	Number of employees with significant security responsibilities who have received required training (Question 6) / Number of employees with significant security responsibilities (Question 3)
Data Source	Employee training records or database; course completion certificates
Indicators	The target for this measure is 100 percent. If security personnel are not given appropriate training, an organization may not be equipped to combat the latest threats and vulnerabilities. Specific security control options and tools are rapidly changing and evolving. Continued training enforces the availability of necessary security information.

	This metric can be correlated with the number of security incidents and the number of patched vulnerabilities to determine whether an increase in the number of trained security staff is related to, and facilitates, a reduction in certain types of incidents and open vulnerabilities.

Comments: Questions 1 and 2 are used to gauge the reliability of the information for this metric. Roles and responsibilities must be defined in policy and procedures, and personnel identified to carry out the roles. Questions 4 and 5 provide information to help identify any specialized training that personnel need to complete.

If sufficient training of personnel is not provided, Question 7 helps identify why. If the cause of insufficient training is known, management can institute corrective actions to remedy this deficiency.

APPENDIX C—SAMPLE AWARENESS AND TRAINING PROGRAM PLAN TEMPLATE

EXECUTIVE SUMMARY

BACKGROUND

OMB A-130, Appendix III
Federal Information Security Management Act (FISMA)
Specific department and/or agency policy (and other relevant information or rationale that may drive an awareness and training program and plan)

AGENCY IT SECURITY POLICY

Goals
Objectives
Roles/Responsibilities

AWARENESS

Audience (management and all employees)
Activities and target dates
Schedule
Review and updating of materials and methods

TRAINING/EDUCATION

Role 1: Executives and Managers
    Learning Objectives
    Focus Areas
    Methods/Activities
    Schedule
    Evaluation Criteria

Role 2: IT security staff
    Learning Objectives
    Focus Areas
    Methods/Activities
    Schedule
    Evaluation Criteria

Role 3: System/Network Administrators
    Learning Objectives
    Focus Areas
    Methods/Activities
    Schedule
    Evaluation Criteria

. . . and remaining roles with significant IT security responsibilities

PROFESSIONAL CERTIFICATION

> Role 1: IT security staff
> > Learning Objectives
> > Focus Areas
> > Methods/Activities
> > Schedule
> > Evaluation Criteria
>
> Role 2: System/Network Administrators
> > Learning Objectives
> > Focus Areas
> > Methods/Activities
> > Schedule
> > Evaluation Criteria
>
> . . . and remaining roles with significant IT security responsibilities

RESOURCE REQUIREMENTS C	**OST**
Staffing $	xxx
Contracting Support	$ xxx
Facilities (e.g., training rooms, teleconferencing facility)	$ xxx
Media (e.g., server(s) for web- and computer-based material)	$ xxx

APPENDIX D—SAMPLE AWARENESS POSTERS

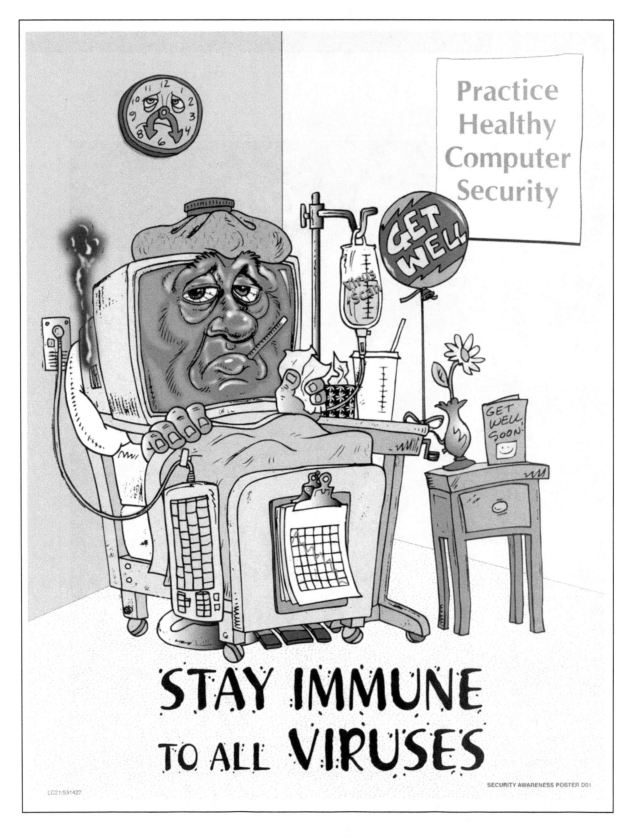

Information Security Tips

1. Use strong passwords.
Any word that can be found in a dictionary is a bad password. Use numbers, letters, punctuation marks, and symbols. (Example: P4$wOrd instead of Password or 43110_2_u instead of hello to you.)

2. Backup your important information.
Save early and save often. ALL important files should be stored on disks or CDs.

3. Use virus protection software.
That means three things: install it, use it, and keep it updated. Schedule your software to automatically scan all of your computer files regularly.

4. Do not keep computers online when not in use.
Either shut them off or physically disconnect them from the Internet connection.

5. Do not open email attachments from strangers,
regardless of how tempting the subject line or attachment may be. Be suspicious of any unexpected email attachment even from someone you DO know because it may have been sent without that person's knowledge from an infected machine or they may be sending an infected file without knowing it.

FOR ADDED SECURITY

6. Use a firewall.
Firewalls are usually software products. Install it and set it up to allow only the services you want. (Example: Email, Web surfing, etc.) Firewalls are essential for those who keep their computers online through the popular DSL and cable modem connections but they are also valuable for those who dial in.

Regional Information Security Workshops are cosponsored by the National Institute for Standards and Technology, Small Business Adminstration, and the National Infrastructure Protection Center InfraGard program.

 National Institute of Standards and Technology • Technology Administration • U.S. Department of Commerce